CABOOSE. L.S.&.M.S.

CHICAGO ROCK ▪ ISLAND AND PACIFIC

ROSITA

CHICAGO ROCK ISLAND AND PACIFIC

VANDOR

92   92

NEW YORK CHICAGO ▪&▪ BOSTON ▪ SPECIAL

Dedicated to Edgar "Bud" Buchardt
whose passion for collecting was the foundation
on which this book was created.

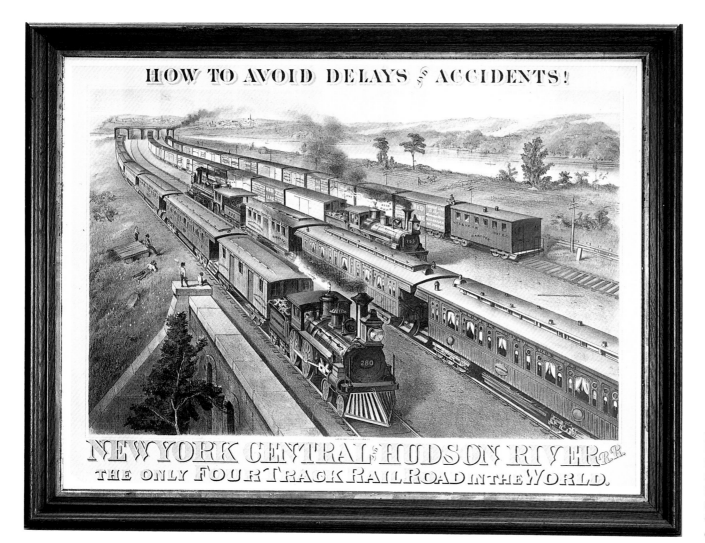

Many cast iron toy trains were patterned after the real trains of the New York Central & Hudson River Rail Road as pictured in this lithograph advertising poster promoting the NYC&HRRR as the only four track railroad in the world. Lithography by Clay, Cosack & Co., Buffalo, N.Y., circa 1890, 21" x 24".

CONTENTS

PREFACE

any years ago, Rick Ralston asked me what I thought about his writing a book on toy cast iron floor trains. Knowing the difficulty of researching this intimidating subject and aware that it would be a monumental task, I advised him to forget it.

    To his credit and despite the odds, Rick was not deterred. The happy result is this book, which serves as a reliable source of information for collectors, dealers and historians.

    Cast Iron Floor Trains appears after years of persistent study, making this book a valuable contribution to antique toy history. There is a new respect and appreciation for cast iron floor trains because many have been elevated from being mere toys to now being considered an American art form. For example, an 1880 toy train by Carpenter (photograph 70, page 27 herein) is shown in *The Index of American Design*, a respected reference book of decorative arts, published by Macmillan in 1950, at once giving owners of this toy pride of ownership. Trains eligible for this same honor are found throughout this book.

    There has been much confusion regarding the identity of the manufacturers of these toys and the correct assembly of sets. The solutions to these questions are to be found in this book, which gives us the most authoritative guide yet to be published. In addition, the book displays the beauty, diversity and decorative value of available cast iron floor trains.

    A treasure trove of new scholarship, this book is an essential addition to every toy collector's library. Lucky for us, Rick Ralston shares his interest and, best of all, didn't take my advice!

Lillian Gottschalk
Parkton, Maryland
Author of *American Toy Cars & Trucks*
(American Motortoys)

Opposite: Assorted freight cars; all were pulled by cast iron locomotives, even though one is made partially of wood, one of tin and another of steel.

ACKNOWLEDGEMENTS

Many people have supported me in creating this book. Some of the people to whom I owe a debt of gratitude are listed here, in no particular order:

Phillip Lauer for the majority of the fine photographs that grace these pages.

Bud Muth, also for photography.

Kathy Rowley and Susan Richardson Maddox, my assistants, for typing the copy describing hundreds of trains.

Michelle Goode, my love, for her support over the years and her patience with my late hours and weekends at the office to complete this book.

Majorie Ralston, my mother, for nurturing my collecting instincts from a tender age.

Steve Moder and Randy Yeager for "minding the store" so I'd have time to write this book.

Lillian Gottschalk for her challenge to do something interesting with those "boring black trains," for her beautiful book *American Toys Cars & Trucks* as an inspiration and a research reference, and for her most kind preface to this book.

Dale Buchardt for being my antiquing buddy at so many flea markets and toy shows and for helping to build my collection.

Arnold Ulhorn for his enthusiastic support.

Leo Gonzalez for his artistry in making my rough concepts into a beautiful book.

Tim and Frances Officer of For Color Publishing for computer production, photo scans and coordination.

George Engebretson for making my dry factual information readable.

Fred Schlipf for his guidance on making the format useful to collectors.

Anthony Annesse, Ward Kimball, Lloyd Ralston, Yvonne Scantling, and Bill and Stevie Weart for sharing their knowledge, collections and reference materials.

And to all the other collectors, dealers and friends with whom I've shared our mutual interest, just a few of whom are Terry Actipis, Graham Clayter, Gertrude Hegarty, Ed Hyers, Dudley Maddox, Gaston Majeune, Dr. James Nixon, Bob Sheppard, Bob Smith, Hamilton Stern, Richard A. Trickle, Leon Weiss and Frank Whitson.

Opposite: A 19th Century wood and iron locomotive by WELKER & CROSBY puffs a sooty cloud of cotton.

BIRTH OF A COLLECTION

Back in the late '60s, I ran a classified ad in the Honolulu daily newspapers: "Trains Wanted". What I *really* wanted were electric trains, preferably by Lionel, which was closing up shop at the time. What I got was a cast iron floor train, manufactured around the turn of the century.

"My father gave it to me when I was a boy," the caller said, "in 1906."

It was the first one I'd ever seen and, to tell the truth, it was so old I wasn't much interested. But as a one-owner toy train, it was in superb condition; even the passengers' faces held their original paint. I bought it for $25, which seemed somewhat high at the time.

Today, 25 years and hundreds of sets later, I'm hooked on cast iron toy trains. My collecting has taken me to auctions, toy and train shows all over the country, through catalogs dating back more than a century, and into the homes of some of the most persistent collectors in the world. The result is an extensive collection of cast iron floor trains with examples of almost every variation ever made.

After all my searching, that first, one-owner train is still my favorite. Collecting cast iron floor trains has been fascinating and frustrating, all-consuming and completely unpredictable. And it has introduced me to some wonderful people who share my passion—folks who've been invaluable in helping me build my collection and complete this book.

I believe collectors are born, not made. According to my mother, I started before I could talk. "When I'd take you out in your stroller," she told me, "you always slammed your feet down whenever you saw a matchbook lying on the ground. And we couldn't go on until I picked it up for you."

A few years later, I developed a fascination with things mechanical and with old toys in particular. When our neighbors in Montebello, California, were cleaning out their garage, I inherited their kids' cast iron cars and trucks from the '30s. I was in the steel toy stage at the time and, like other kids of the day, beginning to move into the plastic stage. I thought these cast iron models were beautiful. I still do.

Opposite: Nineteenth Century railroad collectibles—leather bound Railroad Gazette 1888, stock certificates, lanterns with various road names and a cast iron toy floor train made by WILKINS.

TRAIN SETS
GROUPED BY MANUFACTURER

In this section, you'll find cast iron floor train sets listed alphabetically by manufacturer. Under each manufacturer, the sets are arranged from smallest to largest.

Very few manufacturers used brand names on their trains. Most of them chose not to promote their names at all, remaining anonymous to both the public and retailers, since goods were sold primarily through jobbers. Accordingly, most of the representative sets here are identified by the name of the manufacturing company rather than by a brand name.

Hubley was one of the few firms to promote a brand other than the corporate name; their toys were sold under the Lancaster brand. But even this brand was later replaced with just the Hubley name, and that's how the manufacturer's trains are listed here.

Pratt & Letchworth, on the other hand, usually mentioned its Buffalo brand name in its catalogs rather than the company name. For that reason, you'll find P&L trains listed as Buffalo here, too. Likewise, trains by Columbia Grey Iron Company are listed under their frequently used brand name, Climax.

Opposite: Large passenger sets by JONES & BIXLER (right), KENTON (middle) and BUFFALO (left).
DICK KAPLAN PHOTO

Previous Pages: A JONES & BIXLER passenger train waits in the station. The middle set is by HARRIS, which was closely copied by KENTON in the front row.

A.C. WILLIAMS COMPANY
RAVENNA, OHIO

In 1866, Adam Clark Williams bought out the foundry and farm tool production business established 22 years earlier by his father. After a fire leveled the foundry, A.C. moved his operation to Ravenna, Ohio, where it still manufactures castings for oil drilling, aviation and other industries.

In the plant, opened in 1893, the company began producing a variety of toys: trains, cars, airplanes, banks and others. A.C. Williams toys were marketed primarily through Woolworth, McCrory's and Kresge's stores until they were phased out in 1938 in favor of the more profitable castings. A limited line of small iron trains was produced from about 1920 to 1936.

1 – A proper tender for this little **USA** locomotive has not been located. Perhaps the shorter of these two gondolas was meant to suffice as a tender. The passenger coach may have come in a set of two coaches rather than with the freight cars, but even so, it's a bit small for the locomotive. 20" long as shown.

2, 3, 4 – All three sizes of these coaches are numbered **60**. Both larger engines are numbered **400**. In 1914-15 the largest car and the largest loco were sold individually at the wholesale price of 84¢ a dozen. Cataloged 1913-15.

2 – No moving wheels, coaches painted one each, red, blue, green
3 – No moving parts, coaches turquoise
4 – Wheels move, coaches turquoise. In 1913 sold for 39¢ retail with 3 coaches. As shown with two coaches, 21" overall.

This short-lived company was started by William R. Haberlin and Timothy F. Hayes, both former employees of toy giant Ives Corp., also of Bridgeport. Established in 1907, AMRC began making trackless floor trains in 1910 under the trademark, "The Bridgeport Line." That mark was also used by Ives. AMRC closed operations in 1912.

This manufacturer's trains are extremely rare. The 0-4-0 example shown here, in fact, is the only one I have located.

20 (*same as 804*) – The only example I've found of trains made by this company. The tender is from a track train but approximately correct except for the flanged wheels.
From a private collection

When it was founded in 1868, Novelty Iron Works produced plows and other implements for the farmers of rural Illinois. The company's name was changed in 1885 when the plant relocated to a new Freeport industrial area called the Arcade Addition. In 1884, Arcade began manufacturing toy coffee mills, then continually added other lines until the late 1930s, when it was making more than 300 different toys.

Arcade began making floor trains in 1901, at first offering only a wrecking car and a piledriver. A complete line of trains appeared in its 1902-03 catalog and was unchanged through 1917. By 1925, Arcade's catalogs were still using the 1902 artwork to illustrate its trains, though all of the larger sets were gone by this time. The wrecking car and piledriver remained. By 1928, no floor trains were listed in the company's catalog. In 1931, however, the company did offer a cast iron locomotive, flat car and crane car with steel trucks and flanged wheels for use on tracks. And by 1936, the catalog featured an assortment of railplanes and "streamlined" trains with rubber tires.

The company's toy production ceased in 1942. Arcade Manufacturing was sold to Rockwell Manufacturing Co. of Buffalo, New York, in 1946.

30 – Nickelplated. Offered in 1903 at $3.25 a dozen wholesale; the same illustration appeared until 1923. Though the loco was illustrated with **512** on the tender, it probably actually carried the number **150** (several known examples with **150**, none with **512**). May have also been sold by IDEAL. 16½" overall. Cataloged 1903-23.

31 – Nickelplated. Attributed to ARCADE. Though the coach looks identical to 30, it has a rivet in the coupler at each end instead of the single center rivet.

32 – Nickelplated. Uncataloged, attributed to ARCADE.

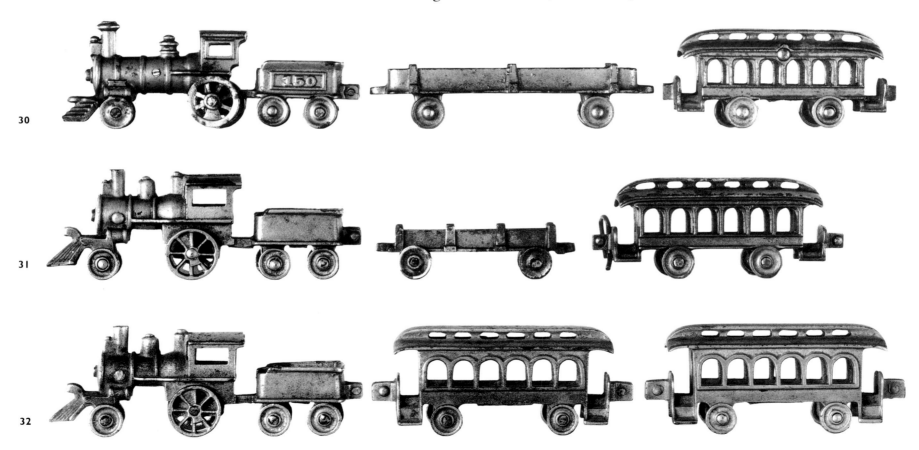

30

31

32

33 — This nickelplated set was offered in 1903 with one or two coaches and the optional addition of a "coal car" (gondola). As shown the wholesale price was $6.00 a dozen. In 1920 the gondola was not offered with this set.

34 — The uncataloged coach in this set is attributed to ARCADE.

35 — Nickelplated set; 2-4-0 locomotive with **808** tender, **SMOKER 375** combination car and **SAPPHO 125** coach, 29½" long. Cataloged 1903.

36 — Nickelplated; 4-4-0 locomotive with **808** tender and **CHICAGO ROCK ISLAND & PACIFIC R.R.** 52" coach. Circa 1910.

37 – Offered at $10.32 a dozen
wholesale. Apparently, few of these
were sold, since this is a very rare set
today. Locomotive and tender black,
box car red with embossed lettering
highlighted in gold (loco missing its bell
and harp), 27½" long. Cataloged by
ARCADE in 1902.

38

38 – Attributed to ARCADE, locomotive measures 6¼" long, coach 5¾", observation car 5¾". Variation: (A) each piece approximately 7" long, more windows than as shown, painted--- red with silver sides, **CENTURY OF PROGRESS** rubberstamped in black on roofs, white rubber tires. Circa 1934.
Hamilton Stern Collection

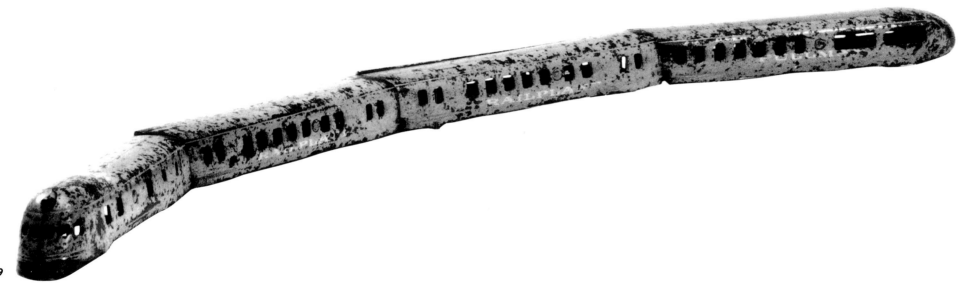

39

39 *(same as 1203)* – ARCADE's No. 382X DeLuxe Express Streamline Train, four-piece articulated set; blue with silver roofs, red on the front apron. Screen printed **DELUXE EXPRESS** in white on the front section, **RAILPLANE** on the two center sections, and **PULLMAN** on the rear section. Also came in all silver with black lettering and was listed as being available in green with silver roof. Units snapped together with a spring wire hook, 32" overall. Cataloged by ARCADE in 1936.

They were billed as "BUFFALO—INDESTRUCTIBLE MALLEABLE IRON AND STEEL TOYS," and were made by Messrs. Pratt & Letchworth.

In toy collecting circles, the name Pratt & Letchworth is more commonly used than the brand name Buffalo, even though P&L's catalogs typically mentioned the manufacturer's name only once and the Buffalo trademark on every page. One full page, in fact, was devoted entirely to the illustrated Buffalo mark.

In 1892, P&L operated under several dba's using the Buffalo name, including Buffalo Home Works, Buffalo Saddlery Hardware Works, Buffalo Malleable Iron Works, Buffalo Grey-Iron Foundry, Buffalo Steel Foundry and Buffalo Brass Foundry.

Various jobber catalogs reveal that Buffalo toy trains were offered from 1890 through 1896. Consequently, production was most likely limited to those seven years. The company's huge vestibule train FFF was a magnificent toy unsurpassed by any other cast iron floor train. In 1890, Pratt & Letchworth acquired the Carpenter toy line and sold both Carpenter and Buffalo trains during the same time period. In 1892, for example, P&L sold a passenger train set under the brand name XL through New York agent Willard & McKee. This set used the popular Buffalo midsize 4-4-0 locomotive and tender with a different coach. An 1896 jobber catalog illustrated a Carpenter set likely produced by P&L.

George S. Crosby, formerly of Welker & Crosby, was hired by P&L in 1899.

The Buffalo Toy & Tool Works that made lightweight pressed steel toys from 1924 to 1941 was unrelated to Pratt & Letchworth.

50

51

52

53

BUFFALO brand trains were distinctive in their use of heavy gauge steel for tenders, freight cars, passenger coaches and wheels.

50 – This set closely resembles trains made by WILKINS, but the wheels, other than the spoked drivers, are all flat steel disks. It's interesting to note that the same basic coach was offered in a four-wheel or eight-wheel version and was even sold mixed in the same set like this one.

51 – Steel disk wheels are used on the steel tender and gondolas and the cast iron caboose. The caboose is filled with a block of wood. I'm not sure if it's original, but it may have been a remedy

for a rather thin casting that was broken too frequently for customer satisfaction. The Marshall Fields 1890 catalog shows this set with one gondola and no caboose priced at $4.50 a dozen wholesale. In 1893, a caboose was added though the price was still the same. The 1892 BUFFALO catalog shows the set with one gondola and the caboose. The tender wheels are described as "bronzed," a term used for a clear tinted shellac or varnish type of finish on bare metal, usually referred to as japanned. In 1890 the Ward & Taylor catalog listed this as a "passenger" train. The 1896 John M. Smyth Co. catalog offered the locomotive, tender and one gondola at the retail price of 39¢. Cataloged 1890-96.

52 – The locomotive uses steel disk pilot wheels and a bolted-in steel carriage for the drivers. The steel cars all use the oversized cast iron wheels which are the same as those found on WELKER AND CROSBY trains. The **P.&L.R.R.** on the gondola no doubt stands for Pratt & Letchworth Rail Road. This set, including two brakemen, could be purchased for 85¢ from Montgomery Ward in 1889. The Marshall Fields 1890 and 1893 catalogs show the set with two gondolas and two figures, priced at $9.00 a dozen wholesale. The tender was stamped

870 N.Y.C.H.R.R.R. The gondolas were stamped with the same road name. 1889-93.

53 – This uncataloged set is all cast iron. The wheels, other than the drivers, are steel. A similar set is illustrated in the 1892 catalog of XL line of iron toys. XL toys are believed to have been made by PRATT & LETCHWORTH. (Half of the pilot is missing from this locomotive.) The coach is pale yellow. The set 25½" overall. Circa 1892.

54

54 – Engine made of cast iron, a tender and coaches of heavy gauge steel, all hand painted with rubber stamped lettering. The wholesale price was $1.25 from Marshall Fields in 1892. Length 45" overall.

55 (*same as 1382*) – There's nothing in cast iron trains that excels the large, handsome and detailed coaches of the largest BUFFALO set (or the comparable KENTON set), with their wet transferred lettering and decorative trim. This combine coach is 14 ¾" long, 5¾" tall and 3¾" wide and weighs 8 pounds.

55

56 – The granddaddy of all cast iron floor trains is this magnificent set made by PRATT & LETCHWORTH and sold under the brand name BUFFALO. Over five feet long and weighing close to 25 pounds, this was not meant for a small child.
From a private collection

CARPENTER TOYS
PORT CHESTER, NEW YORK

This company made floor trains from 1879 to 1896. Francis W. Carpenter first set up shop in Rye, New York, and was one of the first two manufacturers to apply for a patent on a cast iron toy locomotive, filing an application on October 1, 1879—the same date as rival Jerome Secor. After considerable conflict, an agreement was reached, and both men were awarded patents dated June 8, 1880. Carpenter's patent applications, dated May 4 and May 25 of that year, depict a simple train set which was apparently never produced.

Carpenter's was hardly a high volume business. At their peak in 1888, annual gross sales were only $9,274.09! The toys were cast at the Connecticut foundry of Bridgeport Malleable Iron. Company records show that the first train made was the Rapid Freight Train produced in 1879.

A very large locomotive, measuring $21\frac{1}{2}$ inches with tender, was produced during the 1880s, however few are known to exist today. What's more, there are no cars on record which were made to go with this model.

Carpenter moved his operations to Harrison, New York, in 1882. He enjoyed his peak production years there from 1884 through 1888, when he moved again to South Main Street in Port Chester. His company manufactured a clockwork locomotive in 1888 and 1889, though it seems none have survived. In 1890, the business was turned over to Pratt & Letchworth of Buffalo, which manufactured Buffalo brand toys. P&L produced Carpenter trains at least through 1896; some and possibly all were sold under the XL brand name. While Carpenter began making toys once again in 1892, none were trains.

70

FINE IRON FREIGHT TRAIN.

Made entirely of iron. Neatly painted and striped in gilt. A very durable toy, and one that will afford almost endless amusement to children. The cars can be coupled and uncoupled, and loaded and unloaded at will, and drawn about on any surface either in or out of doors. It consists of **a** locomotive, tender and three open cars, as shown in cut. The entire train is packed in a strong wood box.

Per doz... $9 00

70 – This may not be the most sophisticated train made, but it has the distinction of being one of the first in cast iron. Loco patent date is June 8, 1880; tender and gondolas carry a May 25, 1880 patent date. It's not known if a loco carrying the May 25 date was ever made. Francis W. Carpenter's intent was to provide a toy train that was "proof against the usual violence of careless play." The set was offered with three gondolas packed in a strong wood box at the wholesale price of $9.00 a dozen in 1885. Cataloged 1885.

A Carpenter set as illustrated in the 1885 Wholesale Catalog of Meinecke & Co., Milwaukee, Wisconsin.

71

72

71 – Original boxes for cast iron trains are quite scarce. Even one like this, missing its lid and retaining only a fragment of the paper label, adds considerable interest and value to the train set. The brakeman was a separate removable figure—and therefore often lost. Loco carries patent date of JUNE 8, 1880. This set came with just the one gondola. It was also sold under the XL brand name in 1892, with the wheels painted yellow. 16" overall.

72 – Later locomotives made by other manufacturers had the silhouette of the engineer cast into the cab window area, but they never recaptured the charm of this separate standing engineer. An individual brakeman stands in each of the two gondolas. Circa 1880.

73

74

The manufacturer of these two handsome locomotives is unconfirmed, but is believed to have been CARPENTER. Which tenders or cars went with these locomotives is also unknown. The CARPENTER line of toys was sold to PRATT & LETCHWORTH, which had its own line of iron toys sold under the BUFFALO brandname. These locomotives may have been designed by CARPENTER but manufactured and sold by PRATT & LETCHWORTH.

73 (same as 765) – 9 7/8" long.
The pilot is a separate casting.

74 (same as 1045) – 12 1/4" long.
The pilot and front pilot wheels swivel.

75 – Cataloged as the **NO. 2 IRON FREIGHT TRAIN** set with removable brakeman. Circa 1885.

76 – **IRON PASSENGER TRAIN SET, NO. 221**, cataloged circa 1885.

77 – **IRON FREIGHT TRAIN, No. 200**, cataloged circa 1885.

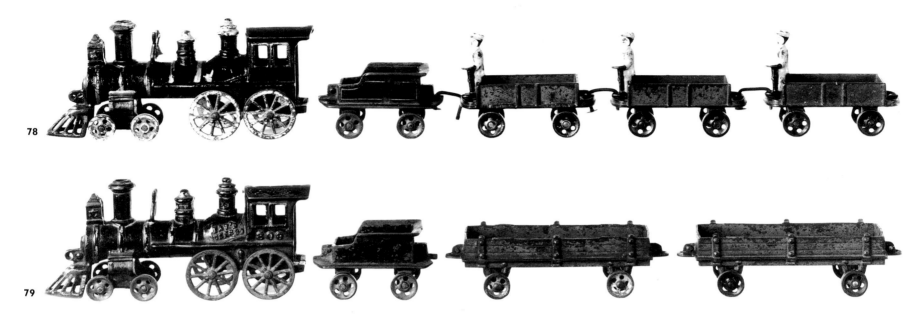

78 – IRON TRAIN NO. 800/2. With three gondolas the number was 800/3. (The correct loco for this set would have the patent date on the side and red wheels. The yellow wheel version was sold under the XL brand name in 1892. Cataloged circa 1885.

79 – These longer gondolas with wood floors are uncataloged and tentatively attributed to CARPENTER, about 31" overall.

80 – CARPENTER's locomotive **800** carrying the patent date June 8, 1880, heads up a passenger set more than 30" long. The engine and tender were cataloged with spoke wheels much like on the coaches, though most are found with the wheels as shown here. These coaches also came pulled by CARPENTER's 2-2-0 locomotive.

Floor trains sold under the Climax name were manufactured by the Columbia Grey Iron Co. Few examples exist today, however, which indicates that only a limited number were produced for a very short period of time.

An 1897 Climax catalog shows several passenger car sets with two sizes of ribbed-sided four-wheel coaches and two sizes of eight-wheel coaches, similar in appearance to Ideal and Arcade trains. Also in this catalog, most of the tenders in various sizes bear the number 475.

100 – Attributed to CLIMAX, this little set has no moving parts. The **42** locomotive is black, the coaches red; 18" overall. Circa 1910.

101 – Attributed to CLIMAX; black locomotive has **45** on the integral tender. On the coaches the clerestory roofs are painted gold, one coach white, one red; about 14½" long.

102 – Black locomotive with red wheels and **650** on the integral tender is attributed to CLIMAX. The dark red coach was cataloged in 1897.

103 – Black locomotive and **475** tender, red wheels. The coach is dark blue with a little gold above the windows, red-orange wheels. Coach also came in yellow, red or the whole set nickelplated. 18½" long with one coach. Cataloged 1897.

104 — Nickelplated set cataloged as set No. 010; with two coaches No. 011. The painted versions were No. 10 and No. 11. Cataloged 1897.

105 — Nickelplated, also available painted, 32½". The manufacturer's price was $126 per gross. After jobber and retailer markups, the price would have been less than $2.00 a set. Cataloged 1897.

DENT HARDWARE COMPANY
FULLERTON, PENNSYLVANIA

The long-established Dent Hardware Co. produced everything from refrigerators to toy trucks between the years 1895 and 1973. Founded by English immigrant Henry H. Dent, the company boasted an excellent reputation for quality craftsmanship.

Dent's first cast iron toys were probably manufactured in 1898. Its floor trains were made from approximately 1900 to 1931, though the Dent No. 10 catalog, circa 1929, shows no trains. The company's toy line was discontinued altogether in the 1930s, when Dent Hardware went back to producing refrigerator accessories and other hardware until its dissolution in November 1973.

120

120 – The electro-oxidized finish on this Dent set has survived better than most, with its bright copper highlights and original varnish finish intact. 41" long with four coaches.

FROM THE **DENT**
TOY SHOPS AT
FULLERTON, PA., U.S.A.

TOYLAND'S

TREASURE

CHEST
REG. U.S. PAT. OFF.

No. 711

Train Set

WHERE LITTLE FOLKS
HAVE HAD THEIR
TOYS MADE FOR
OVER THIRTY YEARS

121

121 – Probably one of the last sets to
be made by Dent in the early 30's was
this petite set meant for a small child.
The integral tender is marked **LVRR** for
LEHIGH VALLEY RAIL ROAD. Overall
length of the 4-piece train set is 23³/₄".

122 – VICTOR engine and tender offered by both HUBLEY and DENT. The coaches with the closed doors are unique to DENT. Cataloged about 1905.

123 – This uncataloged loco—with integral tender spaced way back there, presumably because longer trains commanded more money—is attrib-uted to DENT. The tin coach was found with this locomotive, but it's likely it was made by WILKINS.

124 – This is the most common DENT loco. The ribbed side cars were most often sold in a set of three in red, white and blue. Cataloged about 1905. Also sold in a mixed set of one **N.C.R.R.** gondola, one coach and a caboose.

Sold in 1900 with three coaches and a caboose for 65 cents retail. Circa 1900-05.

125 – This **152** tender with its outboard wheels could easily be confused with the nearly identical Ideal tender. Ideal used a single center rivet while DENT used a rivet on each end in the coupler. Cataloged about 1905

with two or three "flat" cars (gondolas) and with or without a caboose.

126 – This set could easily be confused with similar trains made by HUBLEY, but there are some minor differences. The coaches frequently came in a set of three—red, white and blue—but were also offered all in the same color, or nickel plated. Cataloged about 1905 with one, two, three or four coaches.

127-128 – Two uncataloged sets. Coaches in the foreground are an unusual but attractive color scheme. The nickelplated **P.R.R.CO** tender may be of a later vintage than the locomotive it's with. Circa 1908.

129-130-131 – DENT locomotives can most readily be identified by their unique feature of fixed, non-moving pilot wheels. The front set of pilot wheels on the 4-4-0 move and the rear set are fixed. The patriotic red, white and blue color scheme was popular with DENT. Trains were often cataloged with freight cars and passenger coaches mixed. 129 is 28" long; 131 is 38".

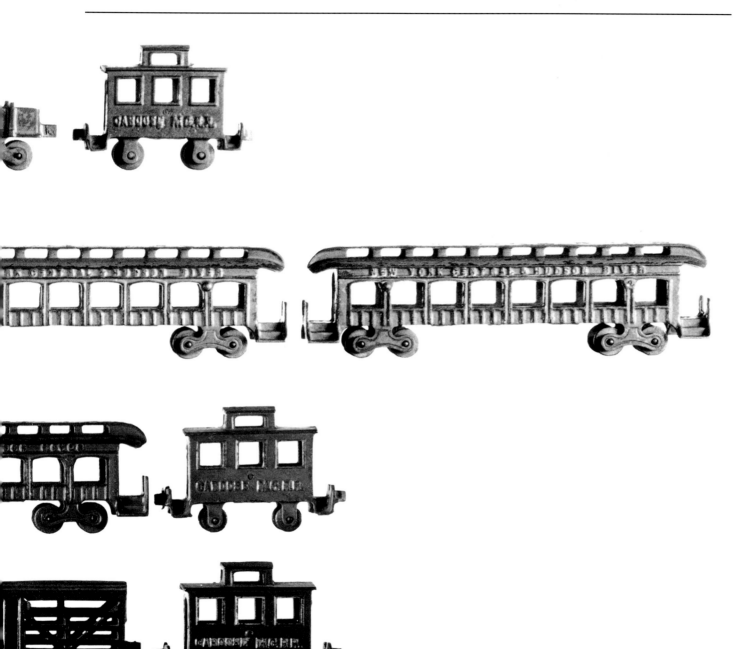

On these 4-4-0 locomotives, the second set of pilot wheels is a solid part of the casting, which is a typical trait of most DENT locomotives.

132 – The popular **999** locomotive and tender pull a red gondola freight set, 39" long.

133 – Red passenger coaches marked NEW YORK CENTRAL & HUDSON RIVER; set 54" long.

134 – This loco was sold heading up an all freight set and an all passenger set and frequently sold mixed. Available with or without a caboose or with only the passenger car. Cataloged 1905.

135 – This set was available as shown or without the caboose or with one stock car, one "flat car" (gondola) and a caboose. Priced at $1.25 a set retail in 1900. Cataloged 1900, 1905.

136 – Attributed to DENT; **BLACK DIAMOND EXPRESS** pulled by a **664** camelback loco with 8-wheel **LEHIGH VALLEY TENDER**, 52½" overall.

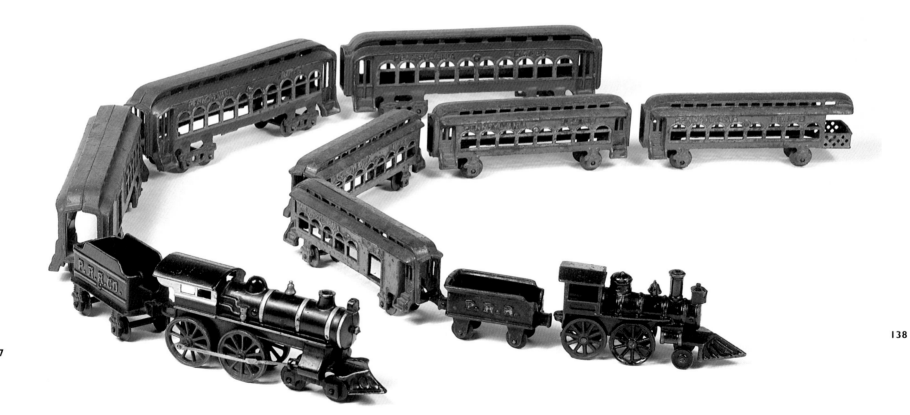

137

138

137-138 – There is no catalog evidence to confirm that these coaches are with the proper locomotive and tender, but they are believed to be correct. The set with brown coaches approximately 50" long, red coach set 52½" long.

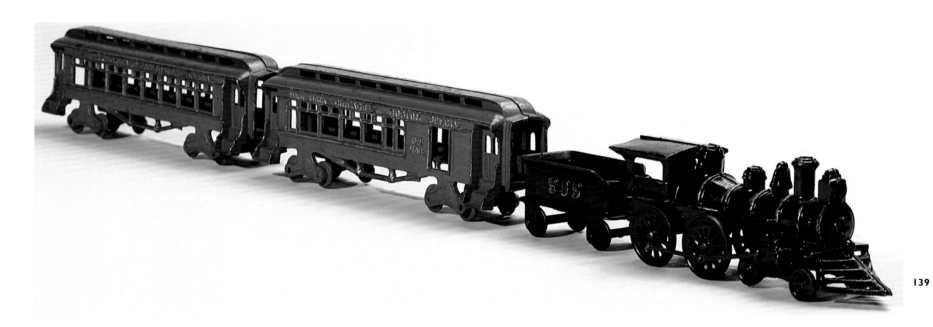

139 – A common DENT locomotive and tender, with a very rare and uncataloged combine and coach, make up this impressive passenger set, 42" long.

139

140 – The **604** locomotive is the largest made by DENT. At first glance it looks exactly like HUBLEY's number **600**, but the DENT does not have skirts over the drivers and, typical of DENT, the second set of pilot wheels is a solid part of the casting. Hoppers also came in a set of red, white and blue, with the common DENT 4-4-0 locomotive with **999** tender.

GREY IRON CASTING COMPANY
MOUNT JOY, PENNSYLVANIA

Grey Iron was one of the companies involved in the National Novelty Corp.—the so-called Toy Trust dissolved in 1907. From 1909 to 1912, this Pennsylvania company was one of three firms which produced floor trains from the patterns of Kenton Hardware Co. of Ohio. At the time, Kenton was under court jurisdiction awaiting reorganization, following the break-up of the second Toy Trust.

In 1920, Grey Iron Casting cataloged a line of cast iron trains which were still quite similar to those built earlier by Kenton. Only very minor changes were made to the castings. The locomotives, tenders and coaches were given numbers, while the names on the coaches were changed. One distinct difference: steel roofs were added on the midsize Ionic and Doric coaches.

Between 1947 and 1983, the Grey Iron number 40 and number 50 locomotives and tenders, as well as the 402 and 403 coaches, were reproduced under the name John Wright, a division of DONSCO in Wrightsville, Pennsylvania. Made from the original patterns, these copies were nevertheless crudely finished. They are detectable by their sandy texture and thin, dull-finish paint. The coaches are usually orange in color—sometimes baby blue—and are often rusted by unscrupulous flea market dealers to look old. DONSCO also reproduced Grey Iron's number 14 trolley, usually painting them black with an orange band.

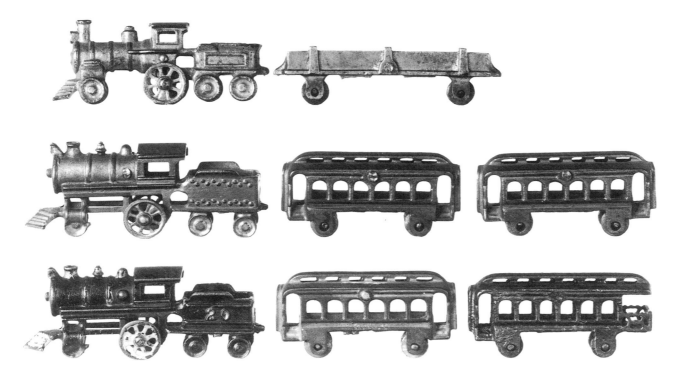

150 – Nickelplated set cataloged by GREY IRON in 1920 as set number **800** with three gondolas.

151 – Copperplated, uncataloged.

152 – Cataloged in 1920 as set **202**, painted with two coaches, red and white, and a blue observation. As shown, 14³⁄₄" long.

153 – What this little set lacks in size, it makes up for in its original, unplayed-with, bright-as-new condition—a condition that collectors like to, but rarely do, find. Cataloged in 1917 with two coaches and one observation car at $3.50 a dozen, the set had gone up to $5.40 a dozen by 1920. Also available nickelplated or copperplated. 25" long.

154

155

156

157

154 – A reproduction painted loco is mixed with the tender, combine and observation car in bright copperplate and the coach in electro-oxidized to show a complete set as it was cataloged. The original set would have been in one finish. GREY IRON trains closely follow the KENTON models, often with only minor variations to the casting. The GREY IRON locos had V-shaped fenders between the drivers, numbers under the cab and numbers on the tenders. Another distinguishing feature: GREY IRON used a coupler on the locomotives to hook to the tender. KENTON's couplers go forward from the tender to the locomotive.

155 – These white, red and blue coaches have sheetmetal roofs on the clerestory, a feature unique to trains made by GREY IRON CASTING CO. The set also came finished in nickelplate, bright copper or electro-oxidized.

156-157 – These are the largest of the sets made by GREY IRON. The **BROADWAY LIMITED** set consists of the number **70** locomotive, tender, combine car, coach and observation car, and measures 5' 3½" in length. Both sets have electro-oxidized finishes. They were offered in 1920 with or without the coach. Cataloged 1920.

THE HARRIS TOY COMPANY
TOLEDO, OHIO

Another member of the National Novelty Corp., or "Toy Trust," the Harris Toy Company produced iron and steel toys, boys' wagons and wheelbarrows from 1887 to 1913, in a factory located at Grand Avenue and Michigan Central Railroad. Frank H. Harris was the company's president, Charles W. West its secretary and treasurer.

Harris catalogs have been located for the years 1903 and 1907. I estimate that toy trains were turned out from 1890 to 1912, when toy production ceased. Following the failure of the second Toy Trust, Harris Toy Co. was bought out in 1907 by Standard Steel Tube Co., also of Toledo.

Kenton Hardware Co. of Kenton, Ohio, copied many of Harris' coaches and some of its locomotives, probably during the period of the Toy Trust. One notable difference: Kenton embossed the lettering on the trains rather than printing it as Harris did. Also, while Kenton at first made the coaches with outboard wheels—just like Harris—it later switched to inboard wheels to reduce the cost of assembly.

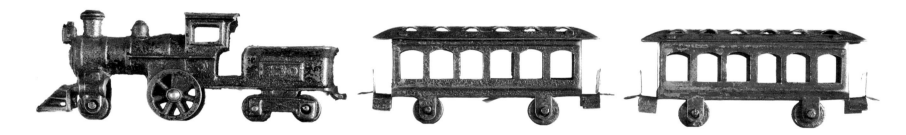

170 – This cheap little dime store set, with its cast iron loco and pressed steel cars, may be one of the rarest sets in this book. But due to its unimpressive size and lack of detail, it wouldn't be valued any more than a larger common set. It proves the point that scarcity alone doesn't have much impact on value. The set is uncataloged but attributed to HARRIS. The tender is numbered **130** with one coach in blue, the other red; 16" overall.

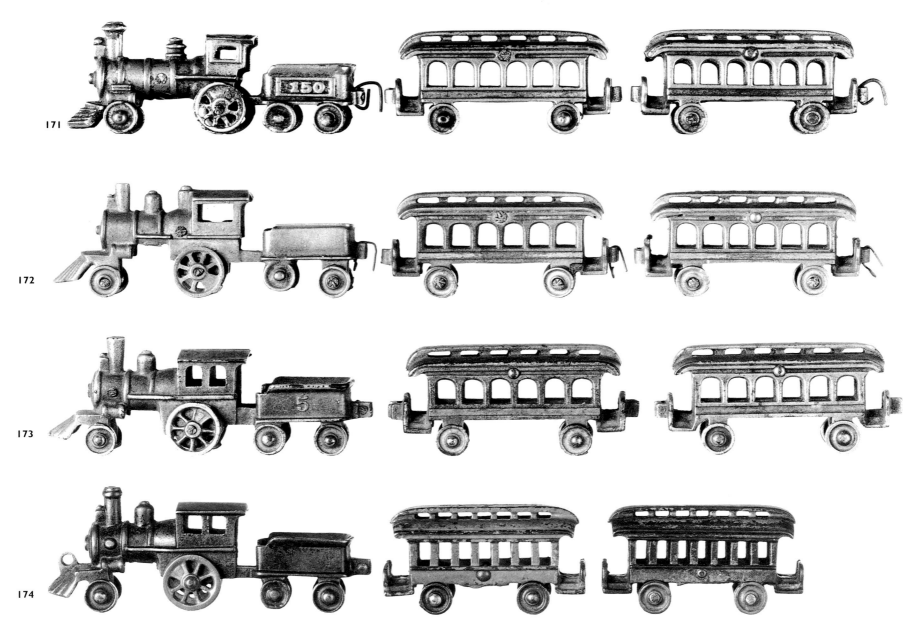

171 – Nickelplated, cataloged by HARRIS in 1903, 15" overall.

172 – Nickelplated, attributed to HARRIS, also came with a black locomotive and one each red, white and blue coaches, 15" overall.

173 – Nickelplated, attributed to HARRIS, 15½" overall.

174 – Black locomotive, red drivers, coaches red, 14" overall, shown in an 1896 retail catalog at 19¢ with one coach. The locomotive cataloged by HARRIS in 1903.

175

176

177

178

175 – Black loco **568**, red-orange coaches, rivets on each end at couplers. Cataloged with one, two or three coaches in either nickelplated or painted finish. Cataloged by HARRIS in 1903.

176 – Nickelplated set, loco **78**, coaches use a single center rivet.

177 – Black loco **568** with tin coaches; complete set consists of three coaches, one each in red, white and blue. Cataloged by HARRIS in 1903 with one, two or three coaches.

178 – Black loco **46**, coaches **87**. These coaches were also sold by JONES & BIXLER and by KENTON as well as HARRIS.

175-178 – All locos have the first set of tender wheels fixed. One rivet is at the front of the boiler and another at the tender coupler except for the **46** in 178, which uses only a single rivet under the cab.

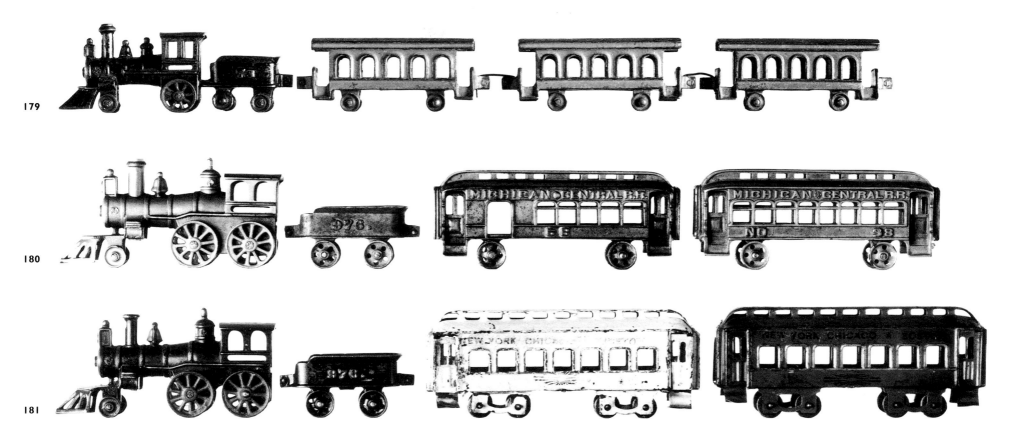

179

180

181

179 – All black **78**, coaches red-orange with dark red roofs, black wheels, 26½" overall.

180 – Nickelplated **MICHIGAN CENTRAL R.R.** set, **976** tender, **68** combine, **NO 98** coach. This set was cataloged by HARRIS about 1903 and offered with a choice of one, two or three coaches, either painted or nickelplated. This set as shown with two coaches; about 29" long.

181 – Cast iron locomotive and tender painted black, red driving wheels. NEW YORK CHICAGO & BOSTON cars are made of pressed steel. In 1903 HARRIS offered this set with one, two, three, or four cars, the set of three being one each red, white and blue.

182

183

182-183 – The nickelplated set in the foreground (183) has two coaches. It also came with one baggage car and a coach like the painted set in the background (182). Both are rubber stamped **NEW YORK CENTRAL & HUDSON RIVER RAIL ROAD**, 31" long. The locomotives are very similar to one made by Ives; the sets are frequently misidentified as such. Circa 1895.

184 – Opposite: Cast iron loco with **999** tender and **NEW YORK, CHICAGO & BOSTON LIMITED** pressed steel coach. This set, with three steel coaches, was the cover illustration on the 1903 HARRIS TOY COMPANY catalog.

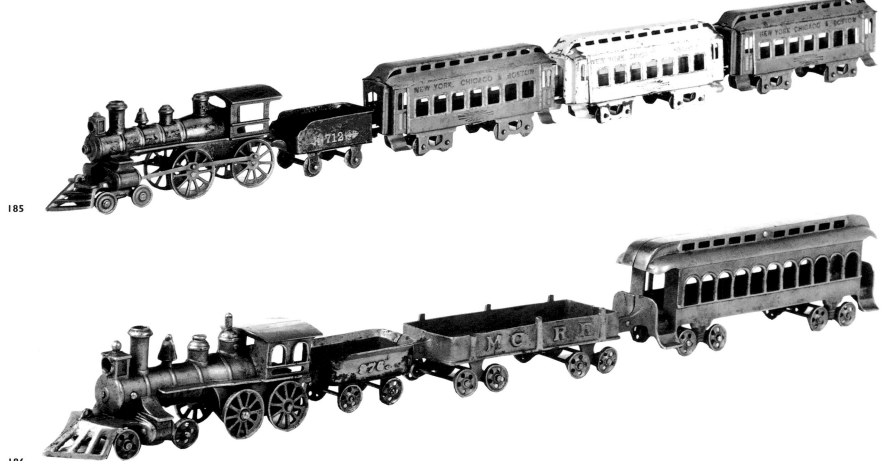

185

186

185 — An uncataloged iron locomotive heads up an otherwise all steel set. The red, white and blue coaches, rubber stamped **NEW YORK CHICAGO & BOSTON**, were cataloged in 1903 with the **712** steel tender but with a different locomotive, 43½" long.

186 — A mixed passenger and freight set made by the HARRIS TOY CO. and finished in nickelplate. Measuring over 37" long. Circa 1895.

187 – A baggage car was made for this set—probably red to go with the white and blue coaches. Sold for 79¢ a set retail in 1896 with a baggage car and one coach. This set 32" overall. Cataloged 1896.

188 – Black locomotive with red drive wheels, **976** tender with **MCRR** gondolas and **CABOOSE M.C.R.R.** in yellow with gold trim, black wheels. Loco missing the valve or whistle off the top of the rear dome (evident in 187).

189 – Typical of HARRIS, no connecting rods were included on locos even as big as this 4-4-0, with **999** tender. Cataloged with two "flat" cars (actually gondolas), with or without a caboose or with three gondolas. Loco missing the valve or whistle off the top of the rear dome (evident in 187). Cataloged 1903.

190 – Cataloged by THE HARRIS TOY COMPANY in 1903 as set **326** with cast iron engine, steel tender and two steel gondolas; number **327** with three gondolas; or number **335** with two gondolas and a cast iron caboose. The catalog illustrations did not show an engineer in the window. It looks like the artwork was altered, possibly for clarity.

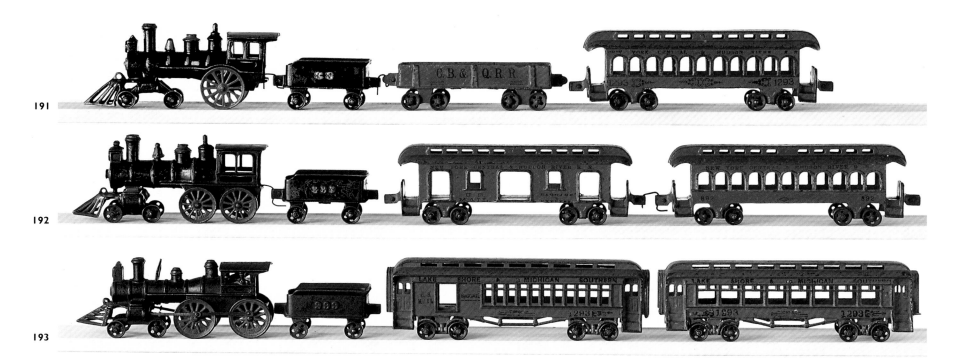

191

192

193

191 – An original set, circa 1895. The gondola rubberstamped **H.T.R.R.** and the coach rubberstamped NEW YORK CENTRAL & HUDSON RIVER R.R. 892. The tender has the number **33** on the left side and **30** on the right, a factory error in assembling the wrong halves.

192 – This is a correct set from about 1895. The locomotive and **999** tender were still cataloged in 1903, but the coaches were no longer offered. 43" long. These coaches were also sold with the 4-2-0 locomotive in 191.

193 – Black locomotive with red coaches rubberstamped LAKE SHORE & MICHIGAN SOUTHERN 1293. Cataloged by HARRIS in 1903 with one, two or three coaches. The catalog illustration did not show an engineer in the window. The set also came nickelplated or electro-oxidized. With two coaches, about 43".

196-197 — These two big beautiful HARRIS sets are identical except for the paint jobs on the coaches. Although the coaches are lettered with the same roadname, the words ROYAL BLUE LINE were dropped when the cars were produced in the mustard colored version. Each set about 52½" long. Cataloged in 1903 with the **917** tender.

198 – Harris' finest: the EMPIRE STATE EXPRESS with ROYAL BLUE LINE coaches in blue-grey, 53" long. Circa 1895.

THE HUBLEY MANUFACTURING COMPANY
LANCASTER, PENNSYLVANIA

Founded in 1893 by John E. Hubley, this long-established firm operated until 1990, marketing toys under the Lancaster brand name from 1906 to 1928 and after that under the Hubley name.

The first Hubley train wasn't a floor train but a cast iron model which ran on an elevated circular track. Power was provided by a clockwork motor mounted in the middle of the track. Patented in April 1893, this flange-wheeled locomotive, tender and single coach was featured on the cover of that year's Hubley catalog. In those days, the company manufactured primarily electric, steam and mechanical toys, but no floor trains.

All that changed in the next decade, when orders by giant jobber Butler Brothers—the nation's largest—prompted the switch from Hubley's original lines to cast iron toys. The 1906 Hubley catalog illustrates six different cast iron floor train sets and two individual locomotives, as well as a pair of clockwork locomotives. While the Hubley name is printed only on the cover, the Lancaster brand is prominent on the cover and on every other page in the edition.

In 1920 the Lancaster line of floor trains had grown to 18 sets. Offered separately were one small steam locomotive, the No. 8 electric-style locomotive and the 23 Skiddoo coaches. In 1928, however, no new trains were introduced in the company's catalog, in which the total line was reduced to only ten sets. Floor trains were all but eliminated by 1930, when Hubley listed only one small cattle train set pulled by a little 2-4-0 locomotive. Finally, the 1933 catalog shows no floor trains at all.

210 – An uncataloged freight set identified by the axles, which are crimped on both ends—a trait exclusive to HUBLEY. The use of passenger coach wheels for the drivers on the locomotive is unusual. Black locomotive, red gondolas, about two feet long. Circa 1910.

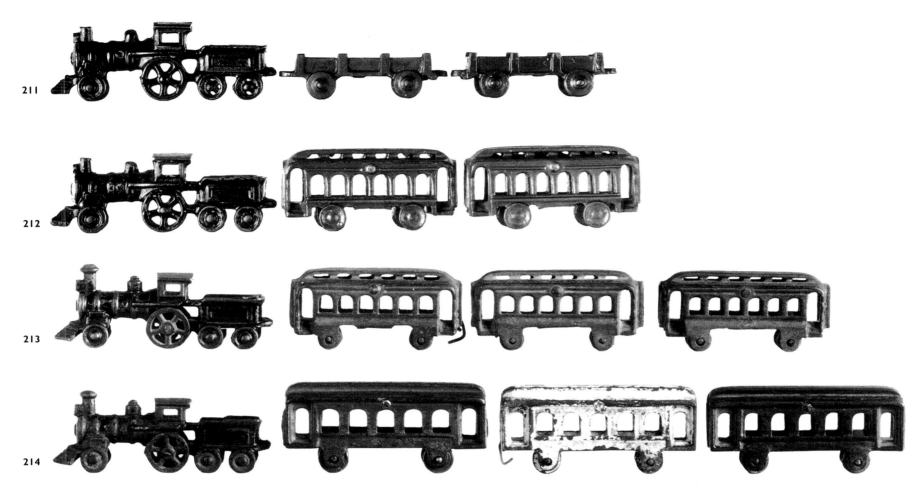

211

212

213

214

211, 212 — There are no moving parts on these little sets. The two halves of each piece are assembled by a single rivet except for the gondolas, which are one-piece castings. The locomotive is black, the cars red. The coach set is 13½" long. Circa 1910.

213 — Locomotive with integral tender and tall stack, red coaches with clerestories. Circa 1910.

214 — Coaches, without clerestories, cataloged by HUBLEY from 1920 to 1932, and probably made as early as 1910. In 1922 the locomotive with one coach was $3.50 a dozen. Coaches commonly came in a set of three: red, white and blue. Circa 1910-32.

233 – The NORMANDIE cars were not cataloged with this smaller locomotive, but it's likely they were sold like this around 1932.

234 – NORMANDIE set available in 1914 and 1915 with a black locomotive and tender and the coaches in red, white and blue or nickelplated, pin couplers; wholesale price $7.80 a dozen. From 1915 to 1919 the set was offered with "automatic" latch couplers, three coaches and an observation car all in red. Wholesale price $1.60 a set.

235 – The nickelplated NORMANDIE set was offered in 1914 and 1915 with the illustration showing the tender in 234, but sold with the tender illustrated here; 36" long.

236 – The **23 SKIDDOO** set was cataloged in 1910 with an electro-oxidized finish at $8.00 a dozen wholesale. These coaches are red with gold trim.

237 – NORMANDIE passenger set, using inboard wheels on the coaches and locomotive but not the tender, was cataloged in 1910 with nickelplated finish at $8.25 a dozen wholesale. In 1911 the price was $7.90 a dozen. These coaches are in one each red, white and blue with gold trim.

238 – Locomotives and cars with the wheels mounted outboard of the trucks generally predate similar models with inboard wheels. This set was available in 1906 with one, two or three coaches. These coaches red with gold trim.

239 – Coaches orange with gold trim. Circa 1906.

240 – Cataloged in 1910 with two NORMANDIE coaches at $6.25 a dozen wholesale. A 1911 jobber catalog shows the same set, but with the first coach only marked **310 GLAWE** instead of NORMANDIE. Loco connecting rods not original. Outboard pilot and tender wheels.

241 – Similar to 240 but with inboard wheels on the pilot and tender. Cataloged with three cars in 1910 at $1.00 a set wholesale in nickelplated finish. Available in 1911 painted or nickelplated at 90¢ a set wholesale. Loco has a notch in the frame between

the drivers (this casting was used both as a push toy and powered with a clockwork motor). Coaches were commonly red, white and blue, wheels mounted inboard of the trucks, pin couplers.

242 – The **444** locomotive (this 48 loco and tender incorrect) was cataloged shown with connecting rods and a choice of one, two or three passenger cars, with the smaller tender 240. The NARCISSUS 44 coaches are the early model with wheels mounted outboard of the trucks, a sheet metal floor and two rivets—one through the clerestory, the other through an underslung bracket. Cataloged 1906.

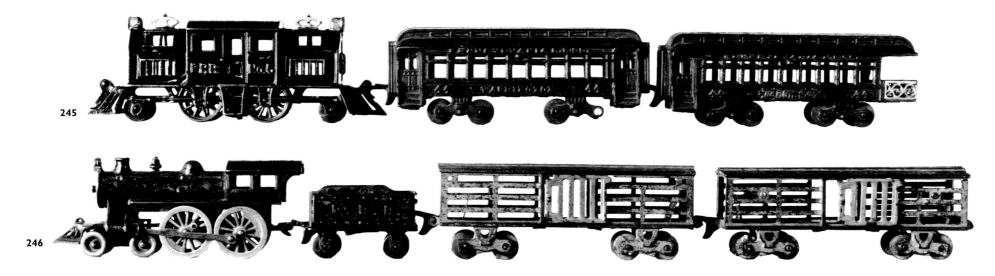

243-244 – These feature 4-4-0 low stack locos. Both were cataloged in 1919 and offered by Sears for $1.87 retail; first shown with "automatic" latch couplers in 1920 and cataloged until 1932. Illustrations always showed two coaches and an observation, although it appears that the sets were normally sold with three coaches and no observation as the observation car is quite scarce. Coaches came in sets of various matching colors and also frequently in red, white and blue.

243 – Pin couplers, 37½" long. Circa 1919.

244 – This set has latch or "automatic" couplers, 28½" long. These apple green **NORMANDIE** coaches, cataloged in 1932, are scarce.

245 – Electric outline loco No. **5** pulling two No. **44** cars, the coach named **WASHINGTON** and the observation car using a different style of lettering: **NARCISSUS**. These frequently

came in a three-car set of red, white and blue, but were also offered in a number of other colors. These two are olive green. Set was illustrated about 1922, available with two or three coaches.

246 – In 1917 the wholesale price was $1.15 per set. The 1920 catalog offered it with one, two or three stock cars and described "automatic couplers," though the artwork still showed pin couplers. Cataloged 1914-19 with pin couplers, 1920 with latch couplers..

247 – The oversized tender in this nickelplated set was designed to go with HUBLEY's larger **857** locomotive, but appears to have been originally sold with this loco.

248 – The "contractor's dump train" was listed at the wholesale price of 99¢ a set in 1914 with three dumping ore cars. The 1917 illustration shows the cars lettered PANAMA.

249 – This "coal train" was cataloged with three hoppers in 1917 at the wholesale price of $1.60 a set. Last seen cataloged in 1920 with only two hoppers at the wholesale price of $2.25 a set. Circa 1917-19 with pin couplers, 1920 with latch couplers.

250 – Cataloged with latch couplers from 1920 to 1929 with two or three coaches. The NARCISSUS observation was sold with the WASHINGTON coach. There was no WASHINGTON observation although there were NARCISSUS coaches. Coaches painted olive with gold trim.

251 – Nickelplated NARCISSUS set with pin couplers, cataloged from 1913 to 1915. In 1913, with four nickelplated coaches, measuring 56" overall, the retail price was $1.98.

252 – The ELOISE coaches were generally cataloged with larger locomotives. The set, as shown here, was cataloged in 1932 with two coaches and an observation car in light blue. These coaches are red with gold trim and use "automatic" latch couplers. Earlier versions had pin couplers.

253 – Offered in 1910 and 1911 with four coaches at a wholesale price of $1.85 per boxed set, finished painted or nickelplated.

254 – This set was offered from 1915 to 1932 with three **NARCISSUS** coaches and the **NARCISSUS** observation at a wholesale price of $2.50 a set. It was listed with two **WASHINGTON** coaches and a **NARCISSUS** observation at a wholesale price of $2.10 in 1919 and $2.50 in 1923; in 1926 the price jumped to $3.75. Coaches were most commonly in a red, white and blue set. In 1932 they were a light blue with pin couplers, circa 1915-19. Latch couplers circa 1920-32.

255 – These are the largest of HUBLEY's rolling stock. HUBLEY's most handsome locomotive, the No. **600**, pulls a pair of **ELOISE 60** passenger coaches. The early models use pin couplers, outboard wheels and two center rivets, one through the clerestory and one in the underslung brace. Cataloged in 1906 in copper oxidized finish with two cars, or painted with choice of two or three cars. The cars were also offered in 1920 with the No. **4** electric outline style loco. Cataloged 1906, 1920.

256 – Locomotive **600**, which has lost its headlight, pulls a set of dumping ore cars. Cataloged in 1910 in nickelplated finish at $1.35 a set wholesale or painted at $1.10 per set wholesale. In 1911 it was offered nickelplated only for $1.20 a set wholesale.

257 – Locomotive **857** uses a sheet metal roof. Hoppers have sheet metal beds with cast iron dumping doors. HUBLEY's 1920 catalog offered this "Coal Train" with a choice of one, two or three cars. It listed "automatic couplers" even though the artwork still showed the earlier pin couplers.

258

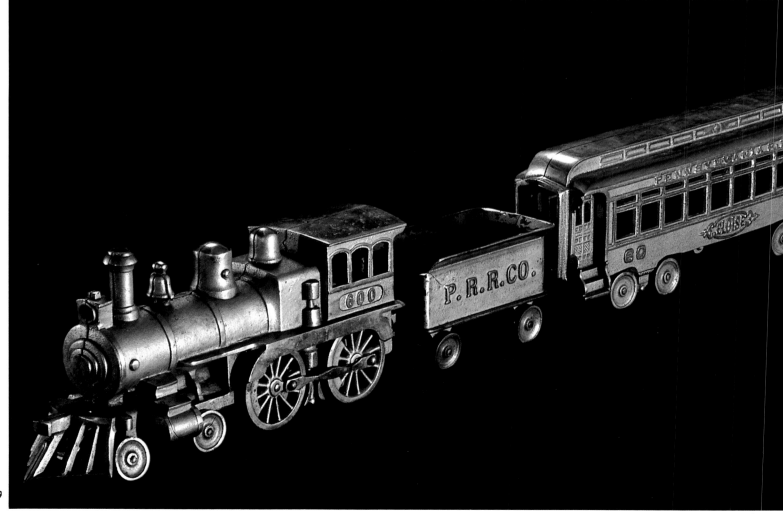

259

258 – HUBLEY's Big **857** loco pulls a set of No. **60** ELOISE coaches in all-American red, white and blue, 53½" overall. These coaches were also cataloged with HUBLEY's largest electric outline locomotive No. **4**.

259 – HUBLEY's big 6-window cab **600** locomotive with a pair of ELOISE **60** PENNSYLVANIA R.R. Co. coaches, all in nickelplate, 41" long. Sold in 1900 for $4.50 retail. Cataloged by HUBLEY in 1906.

IDEAL TOYS
DETROIT, MICHIGAN

Ideal Manufacturing Co. produced cast iron toy trains from about 1894 to 1910. While corporate history is sketchy, we do know that Ideal showed toy trains in 1894 and 1896 catalogs, and also that jobbers listed its trains in catalogs published in 1895 and 1907.

Apparently, Ideal trains were no longer manufactured after the collapse of the second Toy Trust in 1912. There are notable similarities with Dent Hardware trains, however, and the larger Pennsylvania company may have picked up some Ideal patterns for its own use. For instance, both Dent and Ideal used the number 152 on their tenders. At the same time, there appears to have been some transition. Ideal's coaches, for example, all had outboard wheels that moved. Dent coaches had similar outboard wheels, but the ones toward the center of the car were cast solid. On some of these questionable or "transitional" models, both ends of the axles are peened rather than finished with the normal round rivet head on one end.

280 – Nickelplated set; 20"; wholesale price $3.90 a dozen in 1895, $3.00 a dozen in 1899. Cataloged by Ideal in 1896. Circa 1895-99.

281

282

283

284

285

281 — Nickelplated set offered at the retail price of 50 cents in 1901.

282 — Combination set shown in an 1895 jobber catalog with two gondolas and one coach at $7.20 a dozen wholesale, or with three coaches at $8.25 a dozen.

283 — Nickelplated combination set shown in an 1899 jobber catalog with two coaches (no gondola) at the wholesale price of $4.25 a dozen. The **C.R.I & P.R.R.** on this gondola is unusual but appears to be original with this set.

284 — Nickelplated passenger set shown in an 1899 jobber catalog at $7.00 a dozen wholesale with three coaches.

285 — Ideal cataloged this set in 1896 with either one, two or three vestibuled coaches. An 1899 jobber catalog listed the set with two coaches at $7.50 a dozen wholesale. In 1903 a variation of these coaches was offered with cast iron "moving passengers" mounted to a sheetmetal floor that moved to and fro via a crank on the axle. As shown 32" long. Circa 1896-1903.

286

287

286 – This little 26" long set was usually offered with freight and passenger cars mixed. The nickelplated version was either more popular or survived better, since the painted version is less likely to be found today. Cataloged in 1895 in nickelplated finish with one coach and two gondolas at $7.20 a dozen wholesale, or with three coaches at $8.25 a dozen.

287 (*same as 1501*) – Four cast iron commuters—two nickelplated and two handpainted—ride this NEW YORK CENTRAL & HUDSON R.R. coach 1086. The figures are attached to a sheet metal floor that moves back and forth via a wire connected to an axle crank. Cataloged 1903.

288 – Unidentified and attributed to IDEAL, though this also looks much like a HUBLEY or JONES & BIXLER set, nickelplated, 34" long.

289 – All nickelplated set. In 1903 Montgomery Ward illustrated this set with two gondolas only, but described it as having one flat car and one caboose at the retail price of 90¢ a set.

290 – All nickelplated set with the rare MICHIGAN CENTRAL R.R. coach. Cataloged by IDEAL in 1894, offered in painted or nickelplated finish. The same set was shown in a 1907 jobber catalog. Only the gondola has the 5 hole wheels.

291 – The engine and tender have an electro-oxidized finish and the gondolas nickelplated, which is correct as shown in a 1899 jobber catalog. Priced at $8.25 a dozen wholesale.

292 – The finish on the locomotive and tender is electro-oxidized, the coaches nickelplated, which is correct as shown in an 1899 jobber catalog. The set priced at $11.75 a dozen wholesale. About 42" long.

293 – This set has only been found all nickelplated as illustrated here although an 1895 jobber catalog describes the engine and tender as having an oxidized finish. The wholesale price was $8.25 a dozen with one coach.

294

295

294-295 – The cast-in engineer is waving to us with his right hand, although in the catalogs it was his left arm that was up. Set 295 was cataloged in 1896 as train number 139 and was available painted, nickelplated, or gilt. Presumably the gilt finish meant electro-oxidized. These painted coaches are maroon with gold trim, gold on roof of the clerestory. Doors are yellow. Approximately 43½" long.

Set 294 is "as found" although the tender appears oversized and was not cataloged with this set; electro-oxidized finish.

296 – This would be just another ordinary large train set by IDEAL, but note the flanges on the wheels. Floor trains did not run on tracks and did not, as a rule, have flanges on the wheels.

While this may be a prototype experiment by the manufacturer, I presume it was the handiwork of a hobbyist. All the wheels, except the drivers, are machine-turned out of steel. Flanges have been added to the

rear pair of original drivers. The craftsman probably laid his own track, too, since no common toy track could have accommodated the 2³/₈" gauge. This set was originally nickelplated.

297

298

297, 298, 299 — As these sets show, IDEAL typically offered their trains with a choice of painted, nickelplated or electro-oxidized finishes. 297 is painted, 298 has the engine and tender electro-oxidized and the coaches nickelplated, as cataloged. 299 is all electro-oxidized. Sets were offered in various quantities and combinations of cars, often with freight and passenger cars intermixed. The cars could be purchased individually. In 1895 the locomotive and tender, with one passenger car, was priced at $15.50 a dozen wholesale. The longest train, 298, is more than five and a half feet long.

300 — When this animated handcar is rolled along the floor, the action created by an axle crank brings the gandydancer figures to life; 7$^{13}/_{16}$". (Example restored.) Also sold nickelplated.

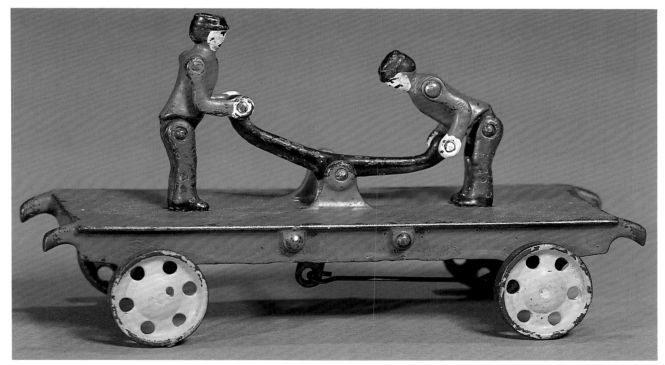

300

299

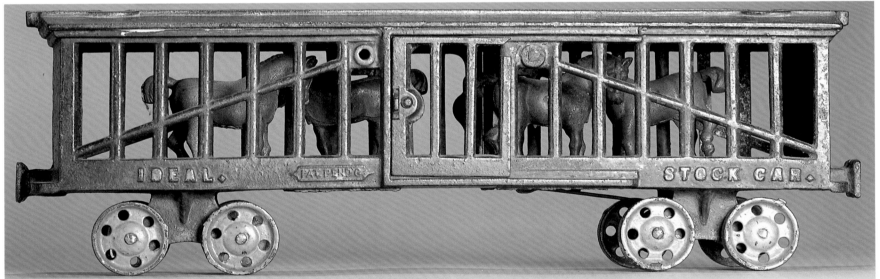

301

301 (*same as 1906*) – Made about 1910, the **IDEAL STOCK CAR** is oversized compared with most other IDEAL trains. Apparently it was meant to be an entertaining toy all to itself. It came painted like this one and also nickelplated or with an electro-oxidized finish. The four cast iron horses are animated via an axle that cranks a connecting rod, causing the steel floor to slide to and fro.

Founded in 1868 and dissolved during the Great Depression, Ives was for a time the biggest toymaker in the U.S. Started by Harry and Edward Riley Ives in Plymouth, Connecticut, the company operated under several names over the years, including Ives, Blakeslee & Williams, E.R. Ives & Co., and Ives Manufacturing. The move to the bustling manufacturing town of Bridgeport was made in 1870.

Ives filed for its first patents on cast iron trains in 1880, the same year as did Francis Carpenter and Jerome Secor. While these two beat E.R. to the patent office, he would soon either own or control the patents of both men.

The Bridgeport company made cast iron train sets from about 1885 to 1901. Eight additional sets with cast iron locomotives and tin tenders and cars are shown in its catalogs from 1910 to 1912 and were probably manufactured from 1909 to about 1915. An 1885 jobber catalog from Milwaukee's Meinecke & Co. illustrates the Ives clockwork locomotive, while an 1895 Montgomery Ward catalog shows the same locomotive, priced at $1.

The Ives, Blakeslee & Williams 1893 catalog illustrates a full line of cast iron floor train sets and individual locomotives with or without clockwork locomotives. The clockwork locomotives were sometimes sold with tenders and sometimes with a single car. More often, they were marketed without tenders, since they hadn't power enough to pull the extra weight. Ives' largest locomotive, vestibule car and box car could be purchased separately. Also shown was a set with two steel passenger coaches marked with the word "Prince," with an open bay area in the middle of the car. These "observation" cars aren't known to exist.

Ives introduced their first clockwork trains to run on tracks in 1901, the same year that Lionel Corp. was formed. Nine years later, the name was changed to Ives Manufacturing and production was dedicated mostly to track trains.

Some of the Ives castings were produced at Watson Ironworks, also of Bridgeport. Watson was owned by George Crosby of the short-lived firm Welker & Crosby, who fashioned floor trains of cast iron and wood. Many other Ives castings were made by Bridgeport Malleable Iron Co.

When E.R. died in 1895, his son Harry took the reins. Harry went on to become a founder and officer of Toy Manufacturers of America. A factory fire at the turn of the century destroyed the Ives collection of 19th Century samples and catalogs. The company filed bankruptcy in 1928 and went into receivership to American Flyer, Hafner Toy Train Co. and Lionel. The latter firm took complete control in 1930, and all remaining Ives trains were moved to Lionel's showroom two years later.

Opposite: Teddy is engrossed with his freight train headed up by a diamond stacked pufferbilly locomotive attributed to Ives. Shown in an 1891 jobber catalog, at a wholesale price of $8.00 a dozen. 25" long.

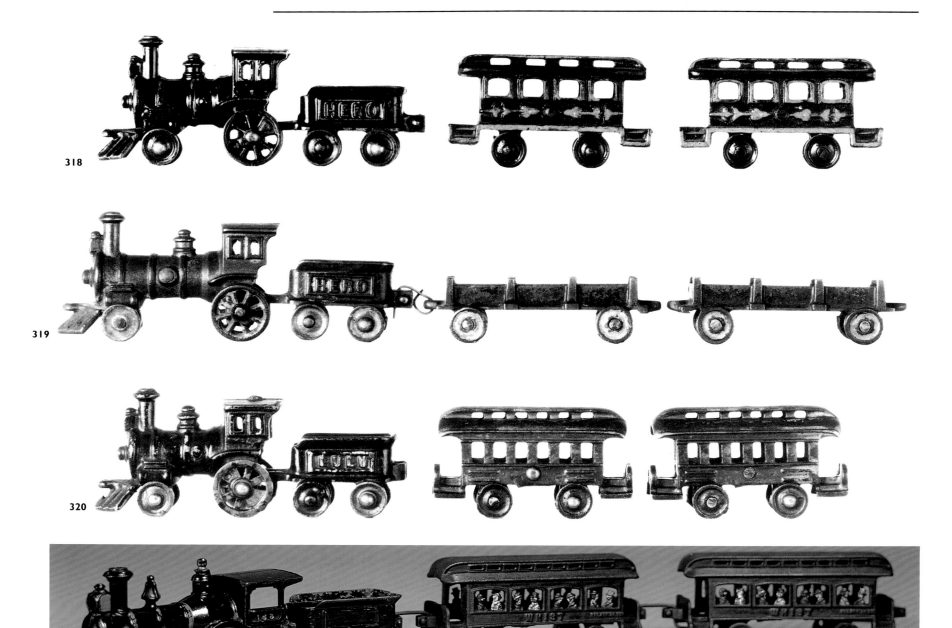

318-320 — These are the babies of the IVES train sets, the longest just 14¼" overall.

318 — The HERO passenger set is illustrated as early as 1889 in a Montgomery Ward catalog priced at $4.00 a dozen wholesale, the same price that IVES offered the set for in 1893 to 1904. The set is all black with gold trim.

319 — Cataloged by IVES from 1893 to 1904 at $2.00 a dozen or with just one gondola at $1.75 a dozen. This set is all black with yellow wheels.

320 — The LULU and her coaches are uncataloged but considered to be by Ives. The coaches red, the locomotive black with gold trim. The drivers are factory installed inside out. All moving wheels are japanned.

321 — These charming little WHIST coaches have a clear-tinted japanned finish over the cast iron; only people and wheels are painted. Perhaps these coaches were named after the card game popular among commuters of the day. Or did the coach builder believed his cars to be so well built as to deserve the name WHIST, which means "to enjoy silence." The coaches carry the patent date of April 30, 1895. Cataloged by Ives in 1902 at $12.00 a dozen wholesale. The set is 29½" long.

These sets are pretty much the same as shown in the 1910 to 1912 IVES catalogs. They are listed as "iron and steel floor trains." Today we generally refer to these lighter weight steel toys as "tin." The sides of the cars, except the gondolas, are printed by lithography. The IVES tin litho cars are difficult to find today. Apparently they did not survive as well as their cast iron cousins.

341 – IVES gave the number 301 to this set when it contained a gravel car (gondola) and a caboose, number 302 with the baggage and passenger car, and 303 with the baggage, passenger and drawing room cars.

342 – Cataloged as number 304 as shown with the gravel, stock car (missing its roof) and merchandise car.

343 – Cataloged as set number 314 with the baggage, passenger and drawing room cars. Without the drawing room cars it was set 312, and with an additional passenger car it was set 316. (Mixed car colors probably not correct within one set.)

344 – As shown, this set was cataloged as number 317. With only a gravel car, merchandise car and caboose number 315, or with two gravel cars and one caboose number 313. (Reproduction tender.)

IVES ADVERTISEMENT

"For wee little chaps, there are trains to be drawn by a string." This is a part of an IVES magazine advertisement that ran in the Saturday Evening Post. December 2, 1911. In the center is Ives' smallest floor train, consisting of a cast iron engine with a tin tender and tin freight cars. Note the way the horses drawing the fire pumper are leaping over the track without the aid of a front wheel. The long hair and dress were appropriate attire for a little boy of that era.

The largest of the IVES sets with iron locos and tin cars, each 30" long.

345 – The coaches with outboard wheels predate 1910. The tender is a reproduction.

346 – The set with inboard wheels was cataloged from 1910 to 1912 with the addition of a combination car and listed as set number 334.

Both sets from a private collection

345

346

347 – The last of Ives' trackless floor trains, this large, handsome set marks the end of an era. The iron loco with tin tender and coaches is 53" long. It resembles the windup track version pulled by the famous No. **40** IVES locomotive. Each coach is 11" long. Set number was 334. Circa 1910-12. *From a private collection*

348 – In 1893 IVES listed this set as the "CANNONBALL TRAIN" and claimed it to be the largest iron train made at 55" long. Wholesale price was $54.00 a dozen, retail price would have been about $7.00 a set.

397

398

399

400

401

397 – Black locomotive and tender, coaches red, white and blue; also available in a nickelplated finish. Cataloged by KENTON 1923.

398 – The 1910 KENTON catalog offers these two coaches with or without an observation, painted, nickelplated or electro-oxidized. Set was available in 1923 either nickelplated or painted.

399 – Cataloged by KENTON in 1914 with one, two or three coaches painted or up to four coaches nickelplated. Also shown as a mixed freight/passenger set with one eight-wheel gondola and one coach or a freight set with one, two or three gondolas and a caboose.

400 – Painted set sold in 1900 for 48¢ retail.

401 – Cataloged in 1905, but with outboard wheels on all units. Circa 1910.

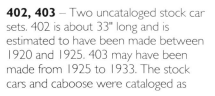

402, 403 — Two uncataloged stock car sets. 402 is about 33" long and is estimated to have been made between 1920 and 1925. 403 may have been made from 1925 to 1933. The stock cars and caboose were cataloged as late as 1933 with another engine and tender. All of the stock cars are orange. The larger caboose is matching orange, the smaller one red but not original to this set; it probably would have also been orange.

404 — Cataloged by KENTON from 1910 to 1927 without connecting rods on the locomotive. Available with one, two or three gondolas and a caboose or with one gondola, one stock car and one caboose; pin couplers; about 48" long.

405 — SANTA FE RAILROAD GRANAGUE coaches in red, white and blue, latch coupler; cataloged in 1910 and shown again in 1927.

406 — ERIE RAILROAD set, nickelplated. Latch couplers, cataloged in 1910 with ERIE on the tender.

407 — PENNSYLVANIA LINE ROUIN coaches, nickelplated, latch couplers, cataloged in 1910, 41" long.

408 — Nickelplated work train, approximately 23¼" long. Cataloged 1905.

409

410

411

412

409 – Attributed to KENTON. **400** black locomotive with red outboard wheels, **LVRR**, black tender and **LEHIGH VALLEY R.R.** red coaches. The combine is number **9167**; the coach is No. **601**. Circa 1905.

410 – Attributed to KENTON. The **400** loco and **P.C.C. & St. L.** tender and **PENNSYLVANIA LINES** coaches have an

electro-oxidized finish. All have outboard wheels. The combine is number **1410** and the coach is No. **1412**. Circa 1905.

411 – Attributed to KENTON. The 4-4-0 locomotive number **178** pulls the same tender and coaches as 410. This set has no finish remaining, but it's likely it was painted. Cataloged 1905.

412 – These coaches carry the same name and numbers as 410 and 411, but are longer as well as having other changes like inboard wheels, lack of protruding couplers, electro-oxidized finish. This set, cataloged in 1914 and 1925 by KENTON, with a third coach, also offered in a painted finish and nickelplated. The catalog illustration shows the locomotive without driving rods.

413 – The **600** KENTON camelback locomotive with stock cars and a caboose are illustrated on a KENTON flyer, circa 1927. 44½" overall. The iron horses were not always sold with the stock cars. Those that were have generally been separated from their cars over the years. The common finish for the horses was copperplate. Painted horses are very rare. Stock cars were cataloged by KENTON in 1923, illustrated with KENTON's big 4-4-0 four-window locomotive. It's doubtful if many of the illustrated sets were sold, as I have only seen this engine and tender with latch couplers which would not go with the pin couplers on the stock cars. The set was titled LAKE SHORE STOCK TRAIN. The tender is marked **L.S.&M.S.** for LAKE SHORE & MICHIGAN SOUTHERN.

414

414 – **600** camelback locomotive with **L.S. & M.S.** (LAKE SHORE & MICHIGAN SOUTHERN) tender, gondola with inboard wheels and a stock car and caboose with outboard wheels. 42" long. Cataloged 1905.

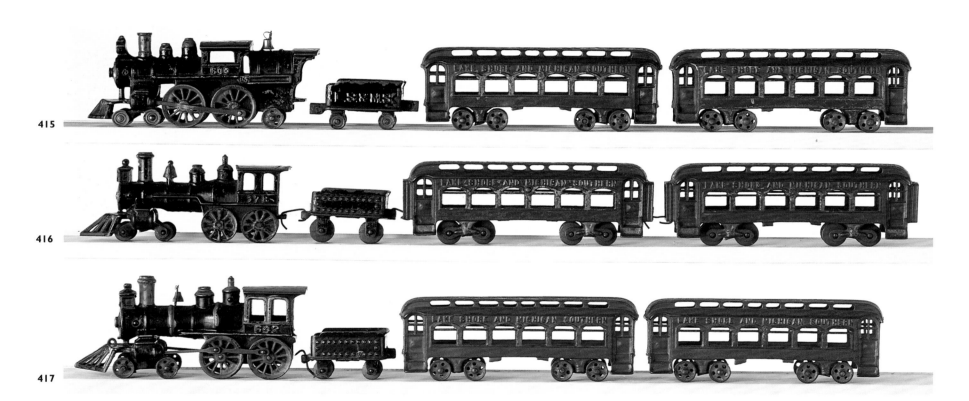

415

416

417

415 – **600** camelback with **L.S. & M.S.** tender; **LAKE SHORE & MICHIGAN SOUTHERN** coaches with outboard wheels.

416 – Coaches are very similar to 415 and 417 but the wheels have gone inboard of the trucks and diaphragms have been added to the ends of the vestibules. The **179** loco and tender also have inboard wheels. The same set also came with smaller diameter wheels on the tender and coaches. The pilot wheels on the locomotive were small in either version. Sold in 1900 with three coaches at $1.65 retail. The 1905 KENTON catalog shows this set with outboard wheels. A 1905 jobber catalog lists this set in nickelplated finish. In 1910 a nickelplated set with four coaches was priced at $1.25 wholesale. About 35" long with two coaches.

417 – A circa 1900 KENTON **642** with coaches the same as 415.

418 – CHICAGO ROCK ISLAND & PACIFIC PULLMAN set, **642** locomotive; coaches have outboard wheels and protruding couplers, circa 1910. This set came either nickelplated, electro-oxidized or painted. In 1900, the set with these coaches in electro-oxidized finish was priced at $3.45 retail. 40½" long.

419 – An uncataloged but original set, circa 1918.

420 – These are the same cars as 419, but with the larger locomotive as cataloged in 1914. Was available painted. 53½" long.

421 – An electro-oxidized finish set, 51" long. Also available painted and with the option of an additional CHICAGO coach or an observation car. Cataloged 1910.

422 – The PANAMA CONSTRUCTION dump car set was cataloged in 1927, but probably offered from 1914 when Panama Canal construction was completed. The cars are known to have come in red or tan and possibly in other colors and finishes.

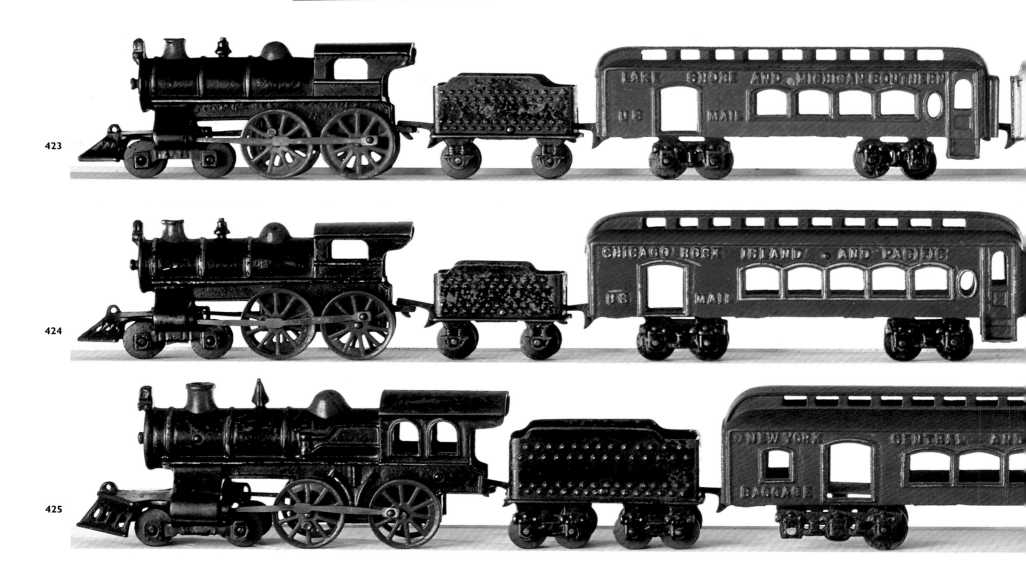

423 – LAKE SHORE LIMITED "Passenger Train," offered with two coaches, either painted or nickelplated or with an observation car painted as shown. Cataloged 1923, 1928.

424 – ROCK ISLAND PULLMAN EXPRESS, offered painted, with an electro-oxidized finish with two coaches, or painted as shown with the observation car. Cataloged 1923.

425 – NEW YORK & CHICAGO LIMITED PULLMAN, offered with the two coaches as shown, either painted or with an electro-oxidized finish. With the addition of an observation car named WASEDA, this set was red, white and blue (some wheels missing). Cataloged 1923.

426

427

426, 427 — Two big KENTON sets, both with an electro-oxidized finish, cataloged in 1910. The EMPIRE STATE EXPRESS set, 426, was sold with a third coach making the whole set a whopping five feet, nine inches long.

428 (*same as 1100*) – KENTON's biggest locomotive is an exact copy of the BUFFALO brand locomotive made by PRATT & LETCHWORTH with a couple of minor exceptions, the most notable being the barrel-like air brake tank underneath the boiler. On the KENTON model it's part of the casting; on the BUFFALO it's a separate wood piece. The BUFFALO was always painted and the KENTON generally was too, though the latter also came with an electro-oxidized finish, as this original loco shows. The electro-oxidized version pulled painted coaches. This tender had its EMPIRE STATE EXPRESS ground off, the finish restored. The loco and tender are two feet long.

429 – KENTON's 1905 version of the **EMPIRE STATE EXPRESS** headed by world speed record holder locomotive **999.** KENTON used the patterns originally created by PRATT & LETCHWORTH and sold under the brandname of BUFFALO TOYS, making only a few changes such as the tender lettering embossed instead of rubber stamped and the coach vestibules enclosed instead of open. Lucky was the child who found this five foot long, 27½ pound set under his Christmas tree.

430-434 – These sets were about the end of the line for cast iron trains made by KENTON or any other company. Clockwork and electric powered trains that ran on tracks were claiming the lion's share of the market. Small, inexpensive cast iron trains, however, could still be sold as "dime store" toys for small children. Ironically, it was at this late date that Kenton began showing enough pride in their toys to mark them clearly with their brand-name. Cars in 431, 433 and 434 are all marked **KENTON** on the outside and **KENTON TOYS, KENTON OHIO** on the inside. All of these locomotives with integral tenders have some, but not all, movable wheels. The little set in 430 measures just 10½" long by 1⁹⁄₁₆" tall. The longest set, 433, is 17" long overall. Generally, the smaller the toys the less care they received, so it's unusual to find them in good original condition. Trains in 433 and 434 were probably never handled by children.

435 – A shining example of a 1933 vintage KENTON set. It owes its fine condition to the fact it sat on the shelf of a KENTON employee and never saw any play time. 26½" long.

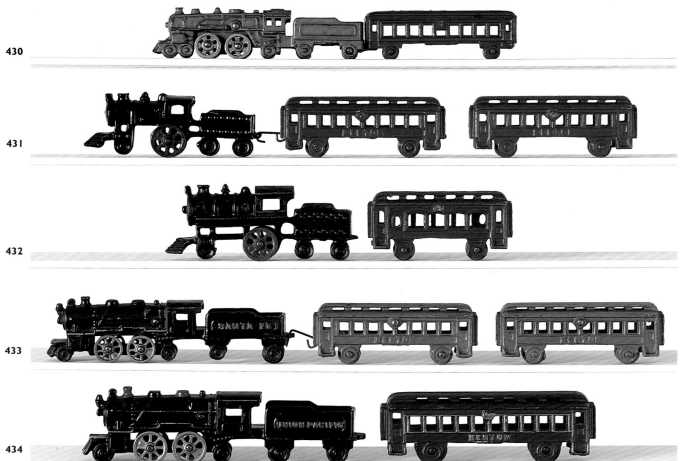

430

431

432

433

434

435

436

436 – A late model steam engine pulls the **NEW YORK CENTRAL ROSITA** Pullman set with an electro-oxidized finish. This set also came painted. Circa 1929

Founded in the early '20s, Kilgore Manufacturing specialized in small NDQ (nickel-dime-quarter) toys which sold in five-and-dime stores during the Depression.

The company joined Andes Foundry Co. and Federal Toy Co. in 1928 to form American Toy Co. Product lines included cap pistols, kites and cast iron cars and trucks. Its iron floor trains were manufactured from approximately 1928 to 1934.

Kilgore operated under the banner "Toys That Last." The company itself wasn't quite so durable, however, and was out of business by the early '40s.

450

451

Iron toy trains just didn't get any smaller than this.

450 – The visible wheels on this loco are cast solid, while movable wheels are mounted inside the pilot and trailing trucks. 12½" overall.

451 – Drive wheels move. Also came as an all-red set.

452 – Most children's toys were lucky if they were even brought in from the sandbox and thrown in the toy chest, so it's unusual when one remains in its original box. This one was made at a time when larger cast iron trains had mostly faded from the market. The "BILLY BOY" set used the inside of the box to promote the company's "SALLY ANN" toy furniture sets. Circa 1930.

453 – No moving parts, all black. 4¹⁵/₁₆".

454 – All black, assembled with pop rivets, 10⁹/₁₆" overall. Taiwan. Circa 1985.

455 – Reproduced from the original GREY IRON molds. But for the rough sand textured finish, it would be hard to tell this set from an original. These coaches were painted orange, while the original pre-war GREY IRON set had an electro-oxidized or nickelplated finish.

The GREY IRON set came painted too, but the finish was a thick dipped, baked-on paint rather than the thin coat of sprayed paint on these reproductions. The copies were sold under the JOHN WRIGHT label and manufactured by Donsco Co. of Wrightsville, Pennsylvania. Circa 1947-83.

456 – Loco and tender 40 with 402 and 403 coaches all in black with gold trim, unusually crude castings that don't resemble any original old toy, 25" overall. Made in Taiwan. Circa 1985.

457 – Loco 444 is reproduced from a HUBLEY loco, the copy being distinguished by its crudeness in casting and rough sand-textured finish. 9¼" long.

458 – Loco and tender 50 would be identical to the original by GREY IRON except for its sand-textured finish and the lack of any facility for a coupler on the rear of the tender. Manufactured by Donsco Co. and sold under the JOHN WRIGHT label. Circa 1947 to 1983.

459 – Made in Taiwan about 1990, this set is not an attempt to accurately copy anything. The paint on the locomotive and tender is flat black. The castings are attached with Phillips-head screws except for the tender halves, which are welded together. The couplers are separate removable pieces. The locomotive only is 8⁵/₁₆", the coach 8¾" and the observation car 8³/₁₆". The whole set 40" overall. Circa 1990.

SECOR (BRIDGEPORT TOY COMPANY)
BRIDGEPORT, CONNECTICUT

Jerome Burgess Secor was a pioneer in the floor train field, making cast iron trains from 1879 to 1883. He first learned tool making and metalwork in his father's gun shop, then made sewing machines and started a toy sideline in 1873. He closed his shop during the financial panic of 1876 and rented space in the nearby Ives Corp. factory.

On November 21, 1879, Secor filed a patent application as the inventor of the cast iron toy locomotive—even though New York's Francis Carpenter had filed a similar claim nearly two months earlier. A settlement reached the following June awarded patents to both men. Whether it was Secor or Carpenter who was first to market with a cast iron floor train remains a mystery. Secor's first train was a pull toy, Carpenter's clockwork powered.

Secor made only locomotives, all powered by clockwork motors. His most popular model was a nine-inch locomotive available with or without a tender. About 1883, he sold his patent and toy line to Ives Corp. and later produced typewriters and rifle tools.

SECOR's complete line of iron trains is represented here. Locomotives could be purchased with or without tenders.

490 *(same as 1185),* – PUCK loco is 7" long, plus tender.

491 *(same as 1178)* – One of the first ever production cast iron toy trains and SECOR's best seller. Illustrated in the 1879 holiday issue of EHRICH'S FASHION QUARTERLY retail catalog, where it was described as "a perfect representation of a railway locomotive. Will run for a considerable distance upon the floor. Made of cast iron, and has a stop movement, by means of which the machinery can be arrested at any moment. Price, $2.00. The same without tender, Price, $1.75."

Originally a hardware manufacturer, J. & E. Stevens Co. was founded in 1843 by brothers John and Elisha Stevens and incorporated in 1869. Stevens' iron toy production began just after the Civil War, about 1865, specializing in cap guns and toy cannon. The company produced a relatively small line of toy trains between 1880 and the turn of the century, when it reportedly sold its patents to Ives Corp. Stevens & Co. remained in business through World War II, with some operations housed in the original 1840s buildings.

My research on this manufacturer turned up one mystery in a November 2, 1885, letter written in response to a Carpenter Toys' infringement claim. "We bought the patterns from Lockwood Manufacturing Company," it reads, "who manufactured them for a year or so before we purchased the patterns." Were these iron train patterns? Who was Lockwood and what did they manufacture? Stevens & Co. produced only the Big 6 locomotive, though I've uncovered two minor variations. Could one of them be a Lockwood model? The search continues.

Only one style of gondola and one coach style were produced to go with the Big 6. A pattern was made for a caboose, although none were apparently manufactured.

500

501

STEVENS produced a very limited line of cast iron floor trains, only the BIG. 6 loco with minor variations and the gondolas and coaches shown here.

500 – The slender coaches are embossed with **NPR** for the **NICKEL PLATE RAILROAD**. 32" overall.

501 – The gondolas are embossed **U.P.R.R.** for the **UNION PACIFIC RAIL ROAD**.

502 — This **BIG. 6** set by STEVENS is the brass master pattern used to make the impression in the sand molds from which the cast iron pieces were formed. The pattern halves are bolted together for display purposes. It's believed the **PDQRRCo** (PRETTY DARN QUICK RAIL ROAD COMPANY) caboose was never produced.

H. WALLWORK & COMPANY
MANCHESTER, ENGLAND

Cast iron floor trains are exclusively of American origin with just one exception—a limited line made by the British firm H. Wallwork & Company. Wallwork trains are of typical British styling: no "cowcatchers" on the locomotives, no large headlights in front of the smokestacks, and coaches with buffers and chains rather than couplers. Freight and passenger cars have two or three rigidly mounted axles rather than swiveling trucks. Wheels on Wallwork iron trains had flanges but were indeed floor toys not intended for tracks. Locomotives were painted as colorfully as the cars.

520 – The 4-4-0 style locomotive seems to have a gondola substituted for its tender (what child would know the difference). The correct tender is similar to that in 521 and lettered KING EDWARD. The coaches also came in the copper and gold color scheme of 521. About 32" long.

521 – A 4-2-2 style locomotive numbered 1892 with an EXPRESS tender, pulling a short freight train. The gondolas were also made with large, 37mm diameter, disk wheels with four holes and no flanges.

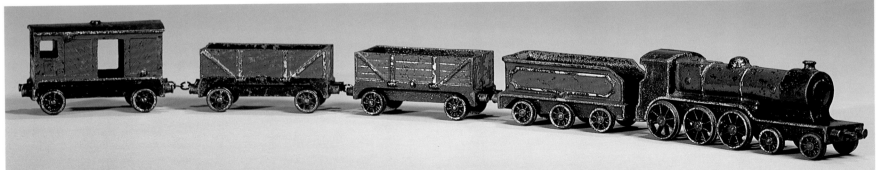

522 – An English cast iron train made by H. WALLWORK & CO. of Manchester, 31½" overall. Circa 1912.

Headquartered at 48 Lexington Avenue, Welker & Crosby produced toys from 1880 to 1890 and patented its first train on November 10, 1885. George S. Crosby was the creative partner, while Welker was the attorney and businessman in this short-lived firm.

Crosby at one time managed both the Watson Ironworks and the Bridgeport Malleable Iron Co.—both located in Bridgeport, Connecticut, and both used by Ives for production of some of its castings. Several patents were issued in Crosby's name and in 1899, he moved to Buffalo, New York, to design toys for Pratt & Letchworth, manufacturers of Buffalo and XL brand trains.

Welker & Crosby cast iron trains are quite distinctive, with locomotive boilers and car frames made of wood and the rest in iron. The company also made clockwork locomotives with or without tenders, as well as train sets to be pulled by a string.

540

541

Both of these sets were made of wood and cast iron, circa 1885-90.

540 – Set pulled by the six-window cab locomotive was patented November 10, 1885. A catalog illustration from about 1886 shows the gondolas embossed with **W.&C.R.R.** much like the tender (tender repainted). The wholesale price was $9.00 a dozen.

541 – An 1890 wholesale catalog shows this train priced at $13.50 a dozen. The tender and both gondolas are pictured with an engineer standing in each, although these examples have no holes in the floor where a figure would have been attached. The tender is repainted and should have outboard wheels to match the gondolas.

James S. Wilkins started his company in 1890 and sold it to Harry Thayer Kingsbury four years later. The name stayed the same, however, until some major corporate changes in 1919. The company was part of both the first and second Toy Trusts, after which ownership reverted to Kingsbury.

Wilkins Toy Co. made cast iron floor trains from 1890 to 1919, when the name was changed to Kingsbury Manufacturing Co., and Harry's oldest son, Edward, spun off his separate Kingsbury Machine Tool Co. As Kingsbury Manufacturing, Harry and his younger son, Chester, made floor trains with cast iron locomotives and steel cars from 1919 to 1926, and continued making toys until 1942. After World War II, Keystone Toy Co. bought Kingsbury's equipment and for a short while produced Kingsbury toys bearing the Keystone name.

Wilkins made some of the finest, most handsome trains in the field. Its long, slender locomotives, particularly the large ones, were undoubtedly the most accurate and close to scale ever produced. Its large coaches and freight cars were the only ones made with articulated trucks.

But the fabled Wilkins quality was no longer evident after the company became a branch of the Hardware and Woodenware Manufacturing Co.—the second Toy Trust. By 1911, none of the big, beautiful sets were offered, and the small coaches were made of steel—as were many of the freight cars. In 1916 only the locomotives were of cast iron, and tenders and cars were all steel, the last of those appearing in the 1927 Kingsbury Catalog.

560 (*same as 1236*) – WILKINS' largest street car, pulled by a 2 horse team; 18½" long. Circa 1895-1900.

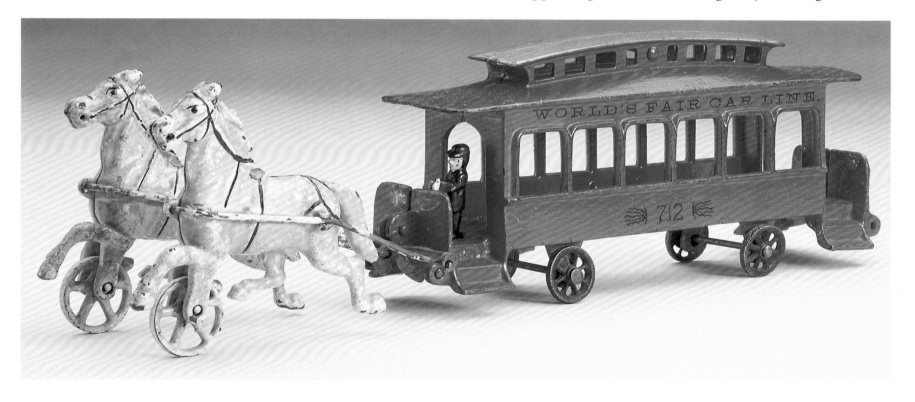

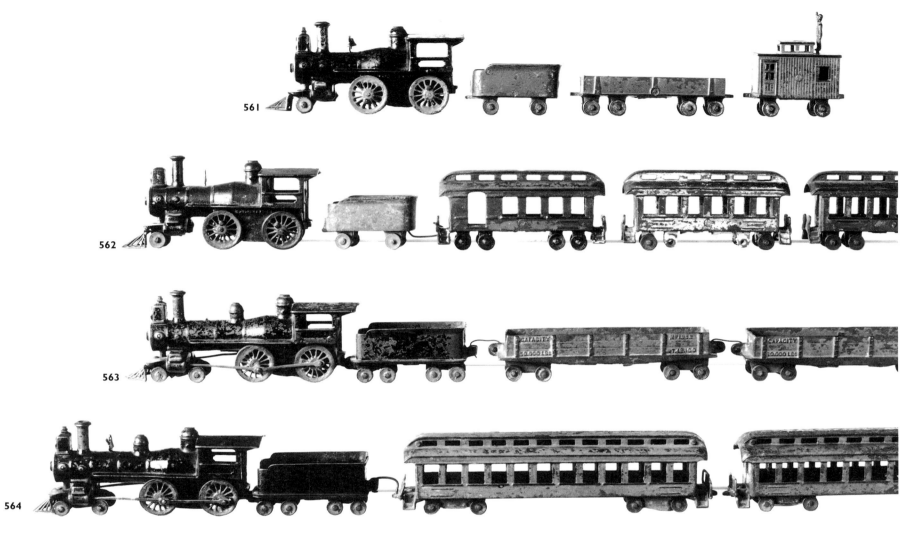

561 – Black loco pulls a tender and freight cars all in red. The gondola came with a brakeman standing inside near one end. (Brakemen weren't secured in place and are usually missing; fortunately this brakeman fits snugly into the holes in the caboose roof or he'd be missing, too.) Cataloged by WILKINS in 1895 with or without the caboose and with one or two gondolas.

562 – Black loco pulls a red tender. Unlike the normal tender in 561, which is cast in two halves and riveted together, this one-piece-casting tender has no rivet. The combination car is in red, the coach in blue and white. Each of the cars has an extra hole in one platform, presumably for a separate conductor figure. Cataloged in 1895 by WILKINS with one coach, with combination car and coach, or with combination car and two coaches. Montgomery Ward listed the set in 1903 at 50¢ retail.

563 – Black loco pulls an eight-wheel tender and red gondolas. Cataloged by WILKINS with or without a caboose in 1895.

564 – Black loco and tender pulling two unmarked red coaches. Cataloged by WILKINS in 1895 with one coach or with coach and combination car. Marshall Fields listed the set in 1890 with one car at $8.50 a dozen or with both cars at $13.50 a dozen.

Engines in 561-564 bear the patent date June 19, '88 (1888) between the drivers and use a pilot that was a separate casting attached with a single rivet. The handrails for the open platforms on the long coaches (564) are separate castings riveted to each end.

565 – This set looks very much like the HUBLEY line, particularly the **NARCISSUS** coach, but it does not have the HUBLEY 44 number. The locomotive and coach were assembled with flat nailhead type rivets most typical of WILKINS; 23½" long.

566 – An unusual set attributed to WILKINS. The long slender coach is more to scale proportions than most toy passenger cars; 28½" long.

567 – The engine and tender, gondola, box car and caboose were cataloged by WILKINS in 1895 as individual pieces. The tank car may have come along in 1896. The box car is most commonly found painted tuscan red. The tank car and gondola may be either red-orange or tuscan, and the caboose is always red-orange. Each car has two little holes where a cast iron brakeman figure would stand. The figure was not shown in the catalog nor has one been located. The entire train is nearly six feet long.

A coal burning locomotive like this one from the late 1800s was an inspiration for IVES, WILKINS and other toy train manufacturers.

568 – One of the large and impressive—but common—WILKINS freight sets, this one is unusual with its original factory hand lettering on the tender and box car and even a **77** on the center dome of the locomotive. Wilkins box cars are occasionally found with **MERCHANT DESPATCH FAST FREIGHT** hand lettered in gold, but the lettering is generally very faint. This is the only example I've seen with the lettering in white and the only lettered tender. The locomotives frequently came with the patent date rubber stamped in gold between the drivers, and occasionally with the date embossed. This locomotive has neither. (The box car is missing its doors).

569 – The coaches have style **A** trucks as shown in passenger train set number 95 cataloged in 1895. The patent date is embossed on the locomotive between the drivers.

570 – In 1895 the combination car and coach were sold individually with style **B** trucks. The patent date is rubber stamped on the locomotive between the drivers.

571 – No combination car is known to exist in the tuscan color to go with these coaches.

The largest of the Wilkins sets are impressive not only in their size but their realistic proportions, closer to scale than most other iron floor trains. Each set is about 54 1/2" long.

572 — A large repainted WILKINS set with lots of charm and an interesting history. It was found with a 1965 letter handwritten by Carl F.E. Weber of Spokane, Washington, the original owner of this train. His letter reads "I received it from Santa Claus when about 6 years old in 1890 and it certainly surprised me and gave me a lot of pleasure. Of course, I shared it with a brother 3 years younger who died about a year later. Another brother came along and soon wanted an interest in it but our father being out of a work a long time fixed it up with kind hearted Santa Claus to rework the train and so Santa gave it to us a 2nd time repainted and it looked better than before." At the time the Webers lived in Chicago, so the set was lettered for the Chicago Milwaukee and St. Paul Railroad.

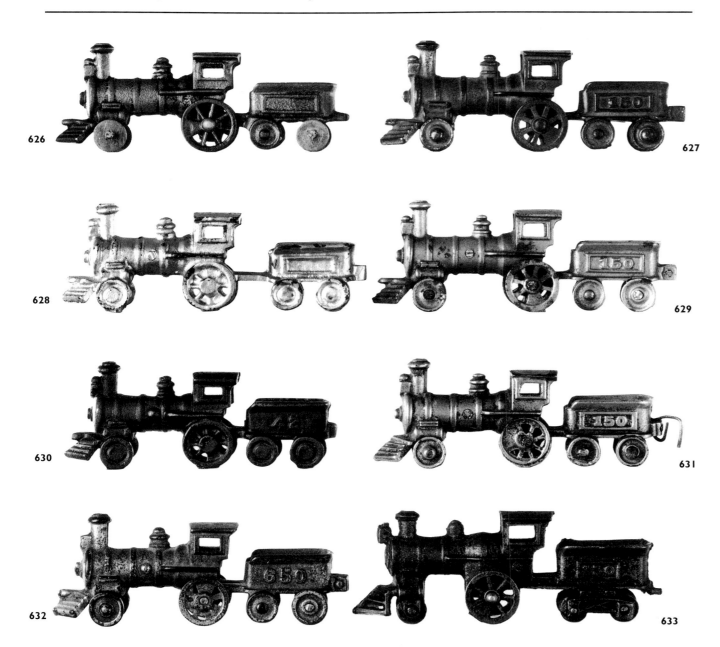

626 – WILKINS
All black, rivet under leading edge of the cab, pilot wheels and rear tender wheels are flat steel. First set of tender wheels do not move, pulled steel coaches, 5$^7/_{16}$". Variation: (A) Cast iron pilot and tender wheels; pulled cast iron coach. Circa 1905-11.

627 – IDEAL
Attributed to IDEAL (possibly ARCADE); 150, nickelplated, rivet under cab window, first set of tender wheels fixed, 5$^{11}/_{16}$". Circa 1895-99.

628 – KENTON
Attributed to KENTON; painted silver, no moving parts, 5$^1/_{16}$".

629 – ARCADE
Attributed to ARCADE (also sold by IDEAL); 150, nickelplated, rivet in center of boiler and rear coupler, first set of tender wheels fixed, 5$^{11}/_{16}$". Variation: (A) opening in cab floor. ARCADE cataloged a similar loco numbered 512 from 1903 to 1923, no example known. (Possibly, the ARCADE loco that was actually sold was numbered 150.)

630 – JONES & BIXLER
Attributed to JONES & BIXLER; 42, black with gold trim, no moving parts, 5$^3/_{16}$".

631 – HARRIS
150, nickelplated; rivet in center of boiler, no front coupler, rear coupler short and round, 5$^7/_{16}$". Variation: (A) Black. Sold in 1902 with one steel coach at $1.50 a dozen wholesale. It was also sold with a choice of two or three steel coaches or with a nickelplated iron coach.

632 – CLIMAX
650, nickelplated; first set of tender wheels fixed, rivet in center of boiler and rear coupler, cab floor open, 5$^9/_{16}$".

633 – HARRIS
Attributed to HARRIS; 150, all black, first set of tender wheels fixed, 5$^{13}/_{16}$". Inside tender embossed 290A on right side, 290B on left side. Casting is unusually thin and light. Believed to have pulled steel coaches.

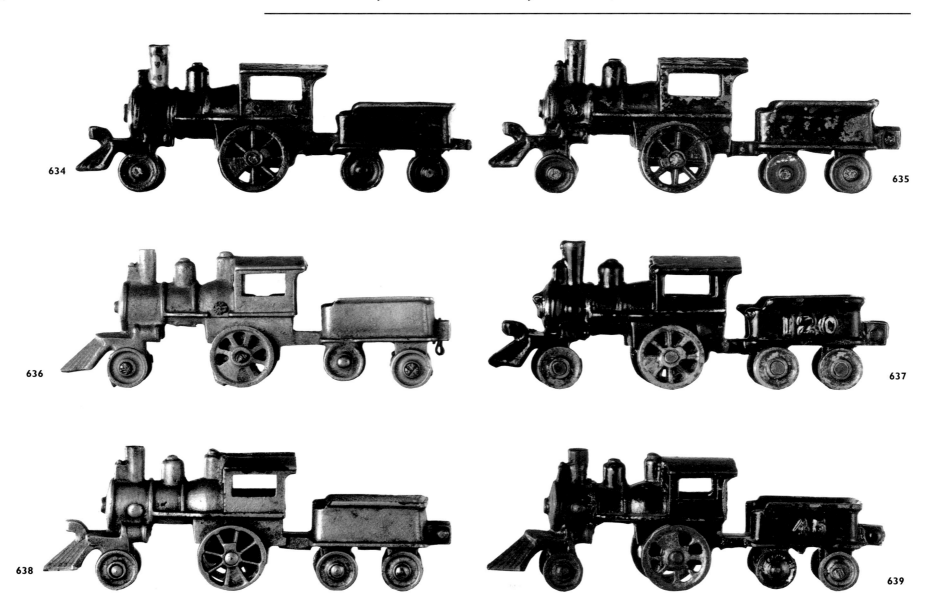

634 – WILKINS
Black with gold bands, red smokestack, first set of tender wheels do not move, front coupler above pilot, single dome, single rivet through cab, 5⅞".

635 – WILKINS
Black with gold boiler bands, black wheels, all wheels move, coupler over pilot, rivets through front of boiler and rear coupler, single dome, 6⅛". Variation: (A) red wheels. Circa 1891-95.

636 – HARRIS
Nickelplated, first set of tender wheels fixed, two domes, single rivet through boiler front just in front of cab, short rounded couplers, no front coupler, 5¾" to 5⅞". Variation: (A) black.

637 – CLIMAX
Attributed to CLIMAX; **120**, black with red wheels, gold trim (example restored); all wheels move, single dome, rivet at boiler front and rear coupler, front coupler over pilot, 5¹⁵/₁₆". Variation: (A) nickelplated.

638 – ARCADE
Nickelplated, all wheels move, two domes, rivet through front of boiler and rear coupler, front coupler above pilot, 6". Variation: (A) black (B) wide shoulder on rear coupler.

639 – JONES & BIXLER
45, black with gold trim, first set of tender wheels fixed and painted black, other moving wheels unfinished, two domes, rivet through front of boiler and rear coupler, 5⅞".

640

641

642

643

644

640 – ATTRIBUTED TO IDEAL
Black with gold trim, no markings,
5³/₄". Copied from IVES (643)
Variation: (A) nickelplated.

641 – IVES
HERO, black with gold trim, wheels are
japanned, rivet in center of boiler and
at rear coupler, 5⁷/₁₆". Cataloged by
IVES in 1893 and 1904, by Montgomery
Ward in 1889.

642 – IVES
LULU, black with gold trim, wheels are
japanned, rivet in center of boiler only,
5¹/₈".

643 – IVES
HERO, black with yellow wheels, rivet in
center boiler and at rear coupler, 5⁷/₈".

644 – IVES
LULU, black with gold trim, wheels are
japanned, rivet in center of boiler and
at rear coupler, 5⁵/₁₆".

645 – HARRIS
Black, red drive wheels, 6".
Circa 1896-1903.

646 – HARRIS
(Also possibly sold by KENTON and
IDEAL in 1899) **5**, nickelplated, rivet
through boiler front and rear coupler,
first set of tender wheels do not move,
outboard wheels, 6". Variation: (A)
black with red wheels, attributed to
KENTON. Circa 1899.

647 – KENTON
5, nickelplated, pilot wheels do not
move, single rivet through cab, inboard
tender wheels, 6". A comparable loco
without the number **5** was cataloged
by KENTON in 1905.

648 – ATTRIBUTED TO HARRIS
Tender broken off, painted black, as is, 4¼".

649 – ATTRIBUTED TO DENT
35, nickelplated, outboard wheels, all wheels move, 6⁷/₁₆".

650 – ATTRIBUTED TO DENT
35, nickelplated, inboard wheels, 6⁵/₁₆". Variation: (A) black with gold trim.

651 – DENT
(Also cataloged by HUBLEY)
VICTOR, 4-window cab, black with red drivers, only the drivers move, 6³/₈". Circa 1907.

652 – HUBLEY
VICTOR, 2-window cab, black with red drivers, only the drivers move, 6⁷/₁₆". Cataloged in 1906 to 1911.

653 – KENTON
Nickelplated, single center rivet under cab window, 6³/₄".

654 – KENTON
Nickelplated, rivet in front of boiler and in tender coupler, 6¹⁵/₁₆".

655 – JONES & BIXLER
46, all black, moveable wheels japanned, outboard wheels, 7¹/₁₆". The 1927 KENTON and JONES & BIXLER catalogs also show the same loco without a number. (Also cataloged by KENTON in 1914, presumably left over J&B inventory.)

656 – HARRIS
568, black with gold trim, pulled either cast iron or steel coaches, 7⁵/₁₆". Variation: (A) nickelplated. Cataloged by HARRIS in 1903. A comparable locomotive without a number was cataloged by HARRIS in 1903 and by JONES & BIXLER in 1905.

657 – WILKINS
46, black with gold trim, inboard wheels, nail head rivet under cab, 7¹/₈". Variation: (A) open area under cab window partially filled like 653.

658 – HARRIS
78, nickelplated, 7³/₈". Variation: (A) black (B) black, pilot wheels and rear tender wheels flat steel.

659 – ATTRIBUTED TO IVES
This example repainted but presumably was all black. First set of tender wheels do not move, 7⁹/₁₆".

660 – CLIMAX
475, nickelplated, first set of tender wheels do not move, 7¹/₈".

653

654

655

656

657

658

659

660

661 – IDEAL
151, nickelplated, 7 3/8". Cataloged by IDEAL in 1894. Variation: (A) painted black. Circa 1895 to 1899. From 1902 to 1923 ARCADE cataloged a similar locomotive with **251** on the tender. No example is known. It could be that ARCADE also sold this **151** locomotive.

662 – CLIMAX
650, black with red wheels, 7 1/8".

663 – DENT
1085, black with red drivers, all other wheels are fixed, 8 7/8". The tender floor is solid. Variation: (A) 3 oval holes in tender floor.

664

665   666

667   668

669 – A.C. WILLIAMS
N.Y.C.R.R. black with gold bell, silver engineer, no moving parts, 5⅜". Circa 1914. Variation: (A) all black, red highlights on tender lettering.

670 – HUBLEY
Black with red drivers, with or without gold trim, tender floor open, no moving parts except drivers, 5⁹/₁₆". Variation (A) tender floor with 3 oval holes. Circa 1919-31.

671 – GREY IRON
20, black, gold trim, orange drivers and pilot, no moving parts except drivers, sloping reinforcement to back of headlight, 5⁹/₁₆".

672 – GREY IRON
Copperplated, no moving parts except drivers, sloping reinforcement to back of headlight, 5⅝".

673 – KENTON
Black with red driving wheels, with or without gold trim, no moving parts except driving wheels, back side of headlight is vertical, 5⅝". The same casting as the WILKINS model in 674 except rivet and axles are roundhead and drive wheels are slightly different. Cataloged by KENTON 1914 to 1923. Shown in a 1912 MEINECKE jobber catalog pulling steel cars.

674 – WILKINS/KINGSBURY
Black with gold trim, driving wheels are painted black, nail head axle and rivet in boiler, only driving wheels move, back side of headlight is vertical, 5⅝". Same casting as the KENTON in 673, though drive wheels are slightly different. Pulled steel coaches. Circa 1912-26.

675 – DENT
Nickelplated, front of boiler does not have protrusion like similar models by KENTON and GREY IRON, 5⁷/₁₆". Variation: (A) electro-oxidized. Circa 1915.

676 – DENT
Black with black wheels, gold trim, same as 675 except for finish, 5⁷/₁₆". Front of boiler does not have protrusion like similar models by KENTON and GREY IRON.

664 – KINGSBURY
10, black with gold trim, no moving parts except drivers, 5". Cataloged by KINGSBURY in 1920-25 with steel coaches.

665 – WILKINS
Black with gold boiler bands, no moving parts except drivers, nailhead rivet and axle, 5¹/₁₆". Tender floor may be completely open or with a center brace.

Sold with steel coaches from 1915 to 1918. Variation: (A) made by KENTON with regular roundhead rivet and axle, no gold on the boiler bands and tender floor partially open.

666 – KENTON
Black, no moving parts, coupler pin hole above pilot, 5¹/₁₆".

667 – HUBLEY
Brown with gold trim, red drivers, no moving parts except drivers, 5⅛". Circa 1914-31. Variation: (A) black with gold trim, red drivers (B) lower ridge on the cab extends half the length of the boiler like 666, black with red drivers, 5¼".

668 – HUBLEY
Black with gold trim, thick nickel plated drivers, no moving parts except drivers. 5⅛".

669

670

671

672

673

674

675

676

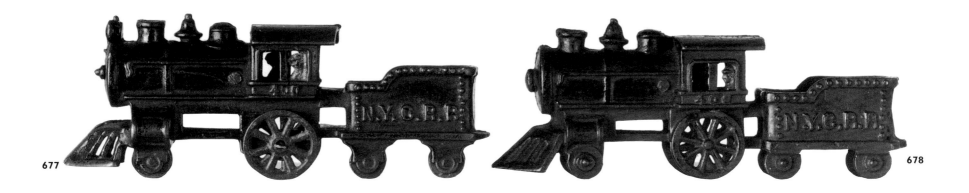

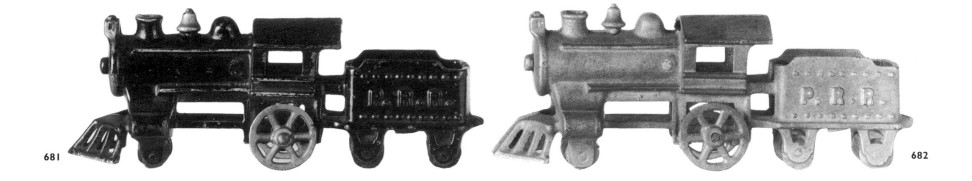

677 – A.C. WILLIAMS
400 on loco, N.Y.C.R.R. on tender; black with gold drivers and bell, silver engineer, no moving parts except drivers, 7¼" – 7⁵⁄₁₆". Variation: (A) red drivers (B) automotive style wheels, fatter with rounded edges used for drivers. Sold in 1914 at 84¢ a dozen wholesale.

678 – A.C. WILLIAMS
400 on loco, N.Y.C.R.R. on tender; black with gold drivers, silver engineer, no moving parts, 7⅛". Circa 1915.

679 – HUBLEY
P.R.R., black, gold trim, red drivers, no moving parts except drivers, 6½" to 6⁹⁄₁₆". Cataloged 1921 without any cars.

680 – HUBLEY
P.R.R, all black, no moving parts except driver (drivers are incorrect on this example; should be same as 679); note vertical support member underneath boiler, 6⅜". Variation: (A) 6⅝", distance between loco and tender is extended, driver spokes are thicker.

681 – HUBLEY
P.R.R., black with gold trim, six-spoke nickelplated drivers, no moving parts

except drivers, tender floor is open, 7⅛". Variation: (A) red drivers (B) eight-spoke nickelplated drivers. Cataloged 1921 without cars. Circa 1914-28.

682 – HUBLEY
P.R.R., nickelplated, no moving parts except drivers, three oval openings in tender floor, 7¼". Variation: (A) black with red drivers, gold bell.

683

683 – DENT
Electro-oxidized, pilot and tender trucks are solid, six spoke drivers, 7".

684 –KINGSBURY
30, black with red driving wheels, gold boiler bands and bell, inboard tender wheels, first set is fixed. Nail head rivet through boiler, nail head axle. Uses wood spacers on axle between driving wheels and frame, 6$^{15}/_{16}$". Variation: (A) 12-spoke driving wheels (B) 12-spoke wheels, no wood spacers.

685 – GREY IRON
Attributed to GREY IRON; 30, black with red driving wheels, gold trim. Outboard tender wheels are fixed, 6$^7/_8$". This example is presumed to be a postwar reproduction, but it's not known if it ever was produced before the war.

686 – GREY IRON
30, nickelplated, first set of inboard tender wheels do not move, 7$^1/_{16}$". Variation: (A) copperplated.

687 – KENTON
Copperplated, 12-spoke driving wheels, first set of inboard tender wheels do not move pin coupler, 7$^3/_{16}$". Variation: (A) nickelplated, pin coupler, (B) nickelplated latch coupler, 6$^{15}/_{16}$". Same casting as in 689, though the finish, rivets and axles differ. Cataloged 1914.

684

685

688 – KINGSBURY
30, all black with natural iron finish driving wheels. Eight-spoke driving wheels spread wide on iron shoulders. Pilot wheels are steel, outboard tender wheels do not move, nail head rivet through boiler and nail head axle, 6$^7/_8$". Variation: (A) 12-spoke red driving wheels.

689 – KINGSBURY
Black with red driving wheels, gold boiler bands and bell, nail head rivet to boiler and nail head axle, first set of tender wheels do not move, 7$^3/_{16}$". Variation: (A) 12-spoke driving wheels. Cataloged by KINGSBURY 1920-25.

686

687

690 – GREY IRON
30, black with red driving wheels smoke stack and dome, gold trim on various highlighted areas; outboard tender wheels do not move; regular round head rivet in boiler and axle, 6$^7/_8$".

691 – KENTON
Black with red smokestack, dome and driving wheels; first set of inboard tender wheels do not move; normal round head rivet in boiler and axle. Tender receives a latch coupler (684 through 690 use pin couplers), 6$^{15}/_{16}$".

688

689

690

691

710 – KILGORE
Blue, all small wheels move, drivers
fixed. Tender is a separate piece.
Loco and tender together, 6".
Variation: (A) orange.

711 – KILGORE
Red, nickelplated drivers and tender
wheels move, tender is a separate
piece, 5⁷/₈" overall. Variation: (A) orange
(B) blue with orange tender.

712 – A.C. WILLIAMS
Blue, only nickelplated drivers move,
integral tender, cataloged in blue, red,
green and tan, 5¹¹/₁₆". Circa 1934-36.

713 – KENTON
Green, nickelplated drivers and rear
tender wheels move, integral tender,
6½". Cataloged by KENTON in 1933.

740 – IVES

Black with red-orange tin bogie wheels, driving wheels dark red, gold trim on cab and bell, separate tin boiler bands, loco only 5⁹/₁₆". Tin tender **F.E. No. 1**, with tin wheels red and black, pulls tin cars. Cataloged as IVES No. 300 1910-12.

741 – IVES

Same as 740 except driving wheels are red-orange Red and black tin tender **CHICAGO FLYER**, loco only 5⁹/₁₆" long. Circa 1910-12.

742 – A.C. WILLIAMS

USA, black with red drivers, loco only 5⁵/₁₆". May have been sold without a tender.

743 – HUBLEY OR JONES & BIXLER

Black with red drivers, inboard pilot wheels loco only 7¹¹/₁₆". Tender **P.R.R.** Sold in 1910 with three **23 SKIDDOO** coaches at $8.00 a dozen wholesale. The finish was listed as "oxidized." They are also shown with three **NORMANDIE** coaches at $8.25 a dozen in nickel finish. The locomotive was cataloged without a tender by JONES & BIXLER in 1912.

744 – HUBLEY

3 on sides of headlight, black with red drivers, 6¹¹/₁₆". Sold in 1914 and 1915 without a tender and with other assorted vehicles and horsedrawn toys at the wholesale price of 89¢ a dozen and a suggested retail price of 10¢ each. Variation: (A) nickelplated.

745 – HUBLEY

Black with red wheels, gold trim, outboard pilot wheels, chassis is notched on the left side for a clock-work motor shaft, loco only 7⁵/₈". Cataloged in 1906 without a tender.

746 – KENTON

Black with red drivers, gold trim, 6⁷/₈". Probably sold without a tender.

747 – ATTRIBUTED TO JONES & BIXLER

Black, red drivers, gold trim. Drivers are thin with counterweights. Loco only 7¹/₁₆". The **P.R.R.** tender may be made by HUBLEY. The loco may have been sold without a tender. Variation: (A) may use tender embossed **47**.

742 **743**

744

745

746

747

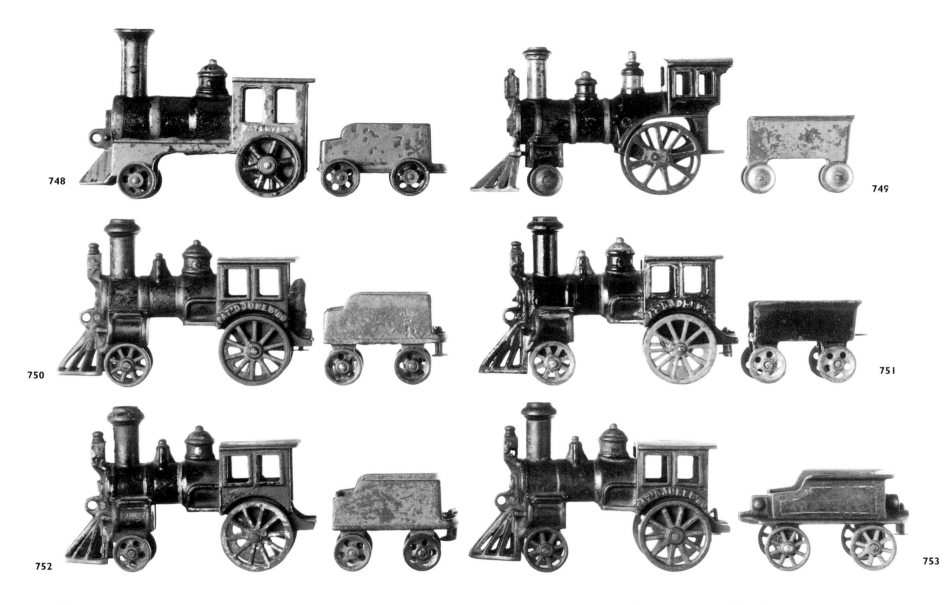

748 – CARPENTER
PATENTED JUNE 8, 1880 embossed on left side of cab. Black boiler with gold band, red cab and frame, loco only 6¼". Tender red PATENTED MAY.25. 1880 REISSUED MARCH 11.1880 embossed on bottom. This is the first production cast iron locomotive. Circa 1880-85.

749 – IVES
Black with red and gold trim, red driving wheels, japanned pilot wheels. The boiler front and pilot are a separate attached casting (the pilot is often broken; check for repairs where

the pilot meets the boiler front), loco only 6⅞". Tender red with gold wheels and handpainted U.P.R.R. Sold with or without tender. The cab floor is solid forward of the driver axle. In the more common clockwork version this area is open to accommodate the motor. Tender may be red, rubber stamped with U.P.R.R. in black, wheels japanned, or black stenciled R.R. in gold, japanned wheels.

750 – CARPENTER
PAT'D JUNE 8 '80 embossed under cab window. Black with smokestack, dome and wheels painted red-orange. Came

with a cast iron engineer. (This engineer lost his head on a midnight run through Sleepy Hollow.) Loco only 6¾".

751 – CARPENTER
PAT'D JUNE 8, '80 embossed under cab window, black with gold trim, red-orange wheels; drivers have a small counterweight; loco only 6¾", tender black with red-orange wheels. The 1884 and 1890 CARPENTER catalogs show the locomotive with this tender and no driver. It is more commonly found with the tender in 750. The 1890 catalog describes it as "best malleable iron train made" and priced at $4.50 a dozen.

752 – XL
Black with yellow wheels and gold trim. No patent date, loco only 6¹¹/₁₆". Correct tender is like 751, but none found with yellow wheels; made by CARPENTER for the XL LINE OF IRON TOYS in 1892.

753 – CARPENTER
Same as 750 except for the larger tender with spoke wheels. Loco only 6¾". Made to go with the larger locomotive, this tender was not cataloged with this loco but may have been sold with it.

754 – IVES
176, black with gold trim, red drivers, japanned pilot wheels; loco only 7$^{15}/_{16}$". Tender **L.V.R.R.**, red with separate cast iron figure. Variation: (A) tender black.

755 – IVES
185, black with gold trim, red wheels; loco only 8$^{1}/_{16}$". Tender black with gold trim and red wheels, no notch for figure. There are a number of minor variations in the shape of the finial on the sand dome. The tender coupler may have a wide shoulder or be long and narrow. Variation: (A) same loco, tender 187, red with japanned wheels. Shown in the 1893 catalog with 185 tender. In the 1904 catalog there is no number on the loco or tender.

756 – IVES
Four-window cab, black with gold trim, red wheels (example restored); loco only 7$^{13}/_{16}$". Tender black with red wheels. Variation: (A) believed to have been made with all wheels nickelplated. Cataloged by IVES in 1904.

757 – STEVENS
BIG. 6, black with red and gold trim, counter balance weights on drive wheels, cab floor extends towards the rear. Loco only $7^{11}/_{16}"$. Tender red with apple green interior.

758 – STEVENS
BIG. 6, black with red and gold trim, no counter balance weights on drive wheels. Cab floor does not extend beyond rear wheels (rivets in smokestack are not correct). Loco only $7^{3}/_{4}"$. Tender **U.P.R.R.** red with apple green interior.

759 – STEVENS
BIG. 6, black with red and gold trim, made without a bell and without a headlight, no counter balance on drive wheels. Pilot is not pierced. The under side of the chassis is cast solid where the above two models have three $^{1}/_{2}"$ diameter openings. The 6 is about half the size of the 6 on the above two models. The locomotive is noticeably heavier than the others. Loco only $7^{3}/_{4}"$. Tender **U.P.R.R.**

760 – CARPENTER
PAT'D JUNE 8, 80 embossed on boiler. A brass cylinder provides compressed air with each wheel rotation, pushing puffs of smoke from a lit cigarette in the smokestack. Sold without a tender. *Gertrude Hegarty Collection.*

761 – CARPENTER
PAT'D JUNE 8, 80 embossed on boiler, black with red wheels, red and gold trim. The engineer is a separate cast iron piece attached by the coupler pin. Loco only $7^{7}/_{8}"$. Tender is red with PAT. MAY 4, 25.1880 REISS'D MAR, 14.82 embossed on bottom. Also sold without a tender. Circa 1880 to 1890.

762 – CARPENTER
Loco same as 761. Tender is black with red wheels, no markings, rear coupler tab is a separate piece.

763 – CARPENTER
Loco is the same as 761. Tender is black with gold striping, red spoke wheels. Circa 1880 to 1890.

757

758

759

760

761

762

763

764

765

764 – CARPENTER
Black with red wheels, red and gold trim, PAT'D JUNE 8, 80 embossed on boiler (repairs to pilot). Loco only $8^{3}/_{8}"$. It's not known if this locomotive was sold with this tender, with one of the other style tenders shown above or without a tender.

765 – CARPENTER
Attributed to CARPENTER; black with red wheel and gold trim. Tender unidentified, $9^{7}/_{8}"$. Variation: (A) pie-shaped counterweights on drive wheels.

766 – HARRIS
Tall valve or whistle on top of dome. Black with red driving wheels. Gold trim. Loco only 8¼" (¼" shorter than the comparable IVES model). Tender 4⁹⁄₁₆" long (¼" longer than the comparable IVES tender). Variation: (A) nickelplated. Frequently the small front coupler has been deleted from the casting on the right side only of the nickelplated version. Circa 1895.

767 – IVES
Made without a bell. Smoke stack cap differs from other comparable models. No paint on this example, but presumed to have been black with red wheels, gold highlights. Locomotive only 8⁹⁄₁₆". Tender **187** does not have the normal embossed rectangle around the number.

768 – IVES
Black with red and gold trim, red wheels. Loco only 8½", tender red. Cataloged by IVES in 1904.

769 – IVES
Black with red drivers, pilot wheels japanned, same loco as 768 except red tender numbered **187**. Variation: (A) first boiler section in front of cab painted gold. Circa 1907.

770 – IVES
178 under cab window, black with red drivers, japanned pilot wheels. It does not appear to have had any gold trim. Loco only 8⅛". Tender **L.V.R.R.** black, slotted for fireman.

771 – IVES
Black with red wheels, red and gold trim (I call this the dachshund model). Loco only 9⅝", tender **187** red.

800 – IVES

Attributed to IVES, black with red wheels, pilot is a separate piece (often missing or incorrectly replaced); loco only 7⁵⁄₈", tender red. Illustrated in an 1890 jobber catalog with two gondolas and priced at $8.00 per dozen wholesale.

801 – IVES

Black, bell and striping in gold, red wheels, separate tin boiler bands; loco only 7³⁄₁₆". Tin tender with tin wheels. Circa 1910-12.

802 – DENT

Electro-oxidized, loco only 7⅛", tender **P.R.R.CO**. Variation: (A) black with gold trim. Circa 1914.

803 – BUFFALO

Black, red and gold trim; loco only 7¼". Steel tender with steel wheels. Tender may be all black with japanned wheels, or black with a red band around the top lip and red wheels, or black with a yellow band and yellow wheels. Circa 1890-96.

804 – AMERICAN MINIATURE RAILROAD

A very rare loco and tender. **AMRR** embossed under cab window. Black with red wheels, steel boiler bands. Loco only 8¼". Tin tender shown here is a track model, but presumably the correct floor model tender would resemble this one.
From a private collection

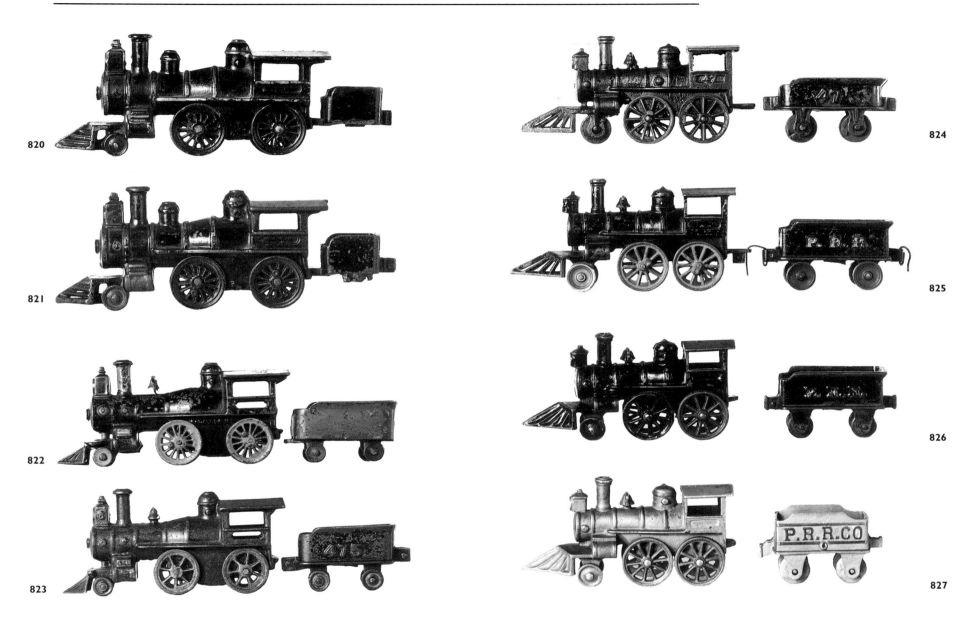

820 – DENT
Black, black wheels, gold trim, pilot is solid, pilot wheels are fixed (may have also come with drivers painted red), 8¹¹/₁₆". Retail price was 90¢ in 1907.

821 – DENT
Black with black wheels, gold trim. Pilot is pierced, pilot wheels rotate, uses a third rivet in tender coupler, 8¾". Variation: (A) Pilot wheels fixed.

822 – WILKINS
Black with red wheels and smokestack, separate steel bell harp. Pilot is a separate attached casting with vertical

bars, although excess casting slag does not allow the pierced pilot detail to show in this photo. PAT. JUNE 19 '88 embossed between drivers, loco only 7¼". Tender red, single center rivet. Variation: (A) black tender.

823 – CLIMAX
Black with red wheels. Clearly a copy of the WILKINS model with different wheels, pilot is solid, 8 on both sides of the headlight, bell is part of the casting. Loco only 6⅞". Tender 475 black with red wheels. Variation: (A) tender P.R.R. (B) nickelplated, no number on the headlight, tender 475 (C) no number

on the headlight, painted black with red wheels, tender 650. Cataloged in 1897, tender shown without a number and large wheels with four holes in each wheel.

824 – JONES & BIXLER
47, black with red drivers, inboard pilot wheels, pierced pilot, loco only 7⅝"; tender 47, inboard wheels. Circa 1910 to 1911.

825 – HUBLEY
Black with red wheels, outboard pilot wheels, pierced pilot, loco only 7⅞"; tender P.R.R., outboard wheels.

Cataloged by HUBLEY in 1906. Variation: (A) silver trim (B) nickelplated, pilot solid, 7¾", by DENT.

826 – DENT
All black, outboard pilot wheels, solid pilot, driving wheels do not have counter weights or areas where connecting rods would attach, loco only 7¹/₁₆"; tender P.R.R., inboard wheels. Circa 1907.

827 – DENT
Loco same as 826 except nickelplated finish. Tender P.R.R.Co. believed to be correct with this loco, but not confirmed.

Locomotives 828 to 837 are virtually identical although made by four different manufacturers. My guess is that the locomotive was first made by IDEAL and then copied by ARCADE, DENT and WILKINS.

828 – ARCADE

Nickelplated, high clearance above drive wheels, pilot is not pierced. Loco only 7⅛". Tender **808**. Circa 1902 to 1925.

829 – DENT

All black with gold trim, pilot pierced, pilot wheels are fixed, loco only 6⅞" to 7¹/₁₆", tender **152** with inboard wheels.

830 – IDEAL

Nickelplated, high clearance above drivers, pilot is pierced, loco only 7¼". Tender **152**. Variation: (A) painted black with red drivers. Circa 1896-1899

831 – DENT

All black with gold boiler bands, solid pilot, fixed pilot wheels, loco only 6¹³/₁₆". Tender **152** with inboard wheels. Also sold without a tender. (Caution - when the tender is broken off from the integral tender model 820 or 821, it may pass for this one, but will measure 7¹/₁₆" and generally not be broken off in a straight line.) Circa 1900 to 1907.

832 – IDEAL

Nickelplated, low clearance above drivers, pilot is pierced, loco only 7¼". Tender **152** with single center rivet, outboard wheels. Variation: (A) painted black with red wheels and gold trim. Circa 1895 to 1901.

833 – DENT

All black, solid pilot, fixed pilot wheels. Loco only 6¹³/₁₆". Tender **152**, outboard wheels, rivets at each end. Tender believed to be correct with this loco, but not confirmed.

834 – ATTRIBUTED TO DENT

Nickelplated, pilot pierced, pilot wheels rotate. Loco only 7⅛". Correct tender unidentified.

835 – WILKINS

Black with red wheels, red smokestack, pierced pilot, pilot wheels rotate. Loco only 7⁷/₁₆". Tender red, cast in one piece. Variation: (A) tender two pieces riveted. Circa 1892 to 1903.

836 – WILKINS

Black with gold trim, red orange smokestack, thin rimmed drivers painted dark red. Loco only 7¹/₁₆". Tender pressed steel, all black. A wholesale catalog from Meinecke of Milwaukee, Wisconsin, circa 1912, illustrates what is believed to be this engine and tender with what appear to be two pressed steel gondolas and a cast iron caboose, neither of which is known to exist.. The drive wheels illustrated are the thick rim model.

837 – WILKINS

Black with red thin rimmed drivers, pilot pierced, pilot wheels rotate, loco only 7¹/₁₆". Tender black with single center rivet.

838 – KENTON
400, nickelplated, inboard pilot wheels, loco only 6³/₄". Tender ERIE, rivets at each end in coupler. Variation: (A) painted black with red wheels, red and gold trim.

839 – KENTON
400, black, red wheels, outboard pilot wheels, loco only 6¹³/₁₆". Tender ERIE. Variation: (A) tender LVRR.

840 – KENTON
400, black with red wheels, inboard pilot wheels, loco only 6³/₄". Tender ERIE, single center rivet. Variation: (A) nickelplated. Circa 1900.

841 – KENTON
400, electro-oxidized, outboard pilot wheels, loco only 6¹³/₁₆". Tender P.C.C.&ST.L. Variation: (A) painted black with red wheels.

842 – KENTON
400, black with red wheels, inboard pilot wheels, loco only 6³/₄". Tender with a rivet detail, no number. Variation: (A) nickelplated.

843 – KENTON
400, nickelplated, outboard pilot wheels, loco only 6¹³/₁₆". Tender L.S.&M.S.

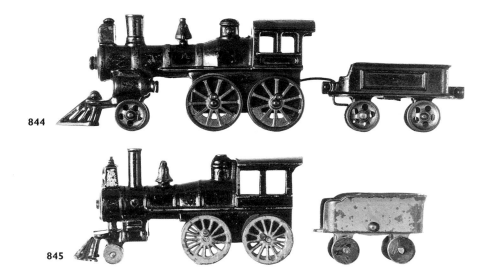

844 – IVES
Black with gold painted boiler bands and bell, japanned wheels, did not use connecting rods; loco only 7³/₄". Variation: (A) red wheels.

845 – BUFFALO
Black with red drivers, gold bell and headlights, steel pilot wheels; loco only 6¹⁵/₁₆", tender red with steel wheels. Variation: (A) nickelplated.

846 – HARRIS
Black with red drivers; loco only 7¹/₄". Steel tender **712** rubber stamped in gold on black as cataloged by HARRIS in 1903, though it isn't known to have been sold with this loco. Cataloged with either two, three or four steel four-wheel gondolas, or one steel gondola and one steel coach, or one steel gondola and one iron coach. Cataloged 1903.

847 – HARRIS
Black with red drivers; loco only 7¹/₄". Tender **976**, black single center rivet, small solid wheels. Variation: (A) tender with 5-hole wheels.

848 – HARRIS
Nickelplated; loco only 7¹/₄". Tender **976** single center rivet.

849 – HARRIS
Nickelplated; loco only 7¹/₄". Tender **976** end rivets. Same as 848 except for tender rivets. Cataloged in 1903 with one, two or three coaches, painted or nickelplated. NOTE: Jones & Bixler cataloged a comparable painted locomotive in 1905 with a **47** tender with outboard wheels, and in 1909 with a **48** tender with outboard wheels.

*The **444** loco is illustrated with connecting rods in the 1906 HUBLEY catalog but apparently wasn't made that way.*

850 – HUBLEY
444 black with gold trim, red drive wheels; frame is notched between drivers to accept a clockwork mechanism, inboard pilot and tender wheels, loco only 9$^5/_{16}$", tender **P.R.R.** Variation: (A) outboard pilot and tender wheels, like 851 but with frame notched.

851 – HUBLEY
444 black with gold trim, red wheels, outboard pilot and tender wheels, loco only 9$^5/_{16}$", tender **P.R.R.**

852 – HUBLEY
Same as 851 except tender is taller.

853 – UNIDENTIFIED
(possibly IDEAL OR ARCADE)
444, nickelplated, all wheels thicker than the HUBLEY'S, drivers are stamped **44**, inside of tender is embossed **44**, no alignment V on the roof, loco only 9$^1/_{16}$".

854 – JONES & BIXLER
48, black, gold trim, red drivers, black pilots, thick rim drivers; rivet at boiler front, in dome and underneath rear coupler tab, 9⅛". Tender **48**, outboard wheels, rivets at each end in coupler.

855 – JONES & BIXLER
48, black, gold trim, red wheels, outboard pilot wheels, thin rim drivers, single center rivet in boiler; loco only 9⅛". Tender **48**, inboard wheels, single rivet. Variation: (A) inboard pilot wheels, thick rim drivers, rivet at boiler front, tender **48**, inboard wheels. (B) inboard pilot wheels, thin rim drivers, single center rivet in boiler, tender **48**, inboard wheels.

856 – WILKINS

Attributed to WILKINS; axles peened on both ends, red wheels and smokestack, gold trim around windows and bell; loco only 9 1/8", tender **918**.

857 – WILKINS

Attributed to WILKINS, black with red driving wheels and smokestack, gold trim around windows, bell, running boards and steam chest. Casting is the same as 856. This one uses nailhead rivets through the boiler and one of the axles. All three axles use a small washer underneath the peened end. Driving wheels are thin and have no point of attachment for connecting rods. Pilot wheels and tender wheels have concentric circles and are smaller in diameter than those on locomotive 856. Loco only 9 1/16" to 9 1/8", tender **918**. May also be correct with a larger **P.R.R.** tender. Variation: (A) brace between pilot trucks and pilot and using round head rivets.

858 – UNIDENTIFIED

Black with red wheels; trim is silver, not gold like most locos. Round guide bars from the cylinders. Front drive wheels are drilled, probably to receive some kind of sliding connecting rods from the guide bars. Two men, an engineer and a brakeman, in each window. Tender embossed **1079**, rear headlight, clevis pin type of coupling. Huge drive wheels are 3 3/8" in diameter. Overall length of engine and tender is 22 1/4".
Ward Kimball Collection

859 – GREY IRON
40 was offered painted, nickelplated, copperplated or electro-oxidized; loco only 6⅞" including latch coupler, tender **40**. (Reproduced 1947-83, see page 131.)

860 – KENTON
Black with red and gold trim; loco only 5⅝"; latch couplers. Variation: (A) electro-oxidized (B) nickelplated. Cataloged by KENTON in 1923.

861 – KENTON
Black with red and gold trim; loco only 5⅝"; pin couplers. Cataloged by KENTON 1914-23.

862 – HUBLEY
Copperplated; loco only 5⅝"; tender **P.R.R.**, pin couplers. Circa 1914-19.

863 – HUBLEY
Black, red drivers, gold trim, pilot wheels fixed; loco only 5¾"; tender **P.R.R.**, latch couplers. The tender is oversized for this locomotive, but that's the way it was cataloged. Variation: (A) six-spoke drive wheels. Sold in 1919 with two **23 SKIDDOO** coaches and one observation car either painted or nickelplated at $8.50 a dozen wholesale. Sold in 1930 with one hopper and a caboose.

864 – HUBLEY
Nickelplated, pin couplers; loco only 7⁹/₁₆". Tender **P.R.R.** with end rivets.

865 – HUBLEY
Black with red wheels; loco only (not including latch coupler) 7³/₈" to 7½". Small tender **P.R.R.** Circa 1915-32.

866 – HUBLEY
Copperplated, loco only (not including latch coupler) 7⁷/₁₆". Tender **P.R.R.** Variation: (A) nickelplated.

867 – HUBLEY
Black with gold trim and red wheels, pin couplers, loco only 7⁹/₁₆". Tender **P.R.R.** Circa 1914-15.

868 – GREY IRON
50 nickelplated, loco only 7³/₄" not including latch coupler which is missing, tender **50**. (Caution: This loco was reproduced in 1947–83; see page 131. Reproduction texture is rough, paint thin, tender has no facility to couple cars.) Variation: (A) copperplated, also came with bulbous weight couplers.

869 – KENTON
Electro-oxidized, latch coupler; loco only 7¹³/₁₆". Variation: (A) nickelplated. Cataloged by KENTON in 1923.

870 – KENTON
Black with red and gold trim; loco only 7¹¹/₁₆" to 7³/₄"; tender missing latch coupler. Same as 869 except painted. Cataloged by KENTON in 1923.

871 – KENTON
Black, loco only 7¹³/₁₆", pin couplers; cataloged in 1914, also shown without connecting rods and sold in sets or just the locomotive without a tender. Same as 873 except tender.

872 – KINGSBURY
Black with red driving wheels, gold bell, nail head rivet in boiler and nail head axles; loco only 7¹¹/₁₆" to 7³/₄"; steel tender. Same loco as 875, except tender is different.

873 – KENTON
Not enough paint on this example to determine the original color, but presumably black with red driving wheels; loco only 7¹³/₁₆"; tender **ERIE**. Same loco as 871 except tender is different. Cataloged painted or nickelplated. Cataloged 1914-23.

874 – JONES & BIXLER (ALSO KINGSBURY)
Black with red and gold trim, did not use rods and has no hole in the steam chest for connecting rods. Loco only 7¹³/₁₆"; cast iron tender (missing one front truck). The 1912 catalog illustration shows this locomotive with what appears to be an Ives tin tender numbered **47**. Variation: (A) nail head rivets and axles, steel box shaped tender by KINGSBURY.

875 – WILKINS/KINGSBURY
Black with red and gold trim, connecting rods, loco only 7¹¹/₁₆". Tin tender may be marked **ERIE**. Circa 1915-26.

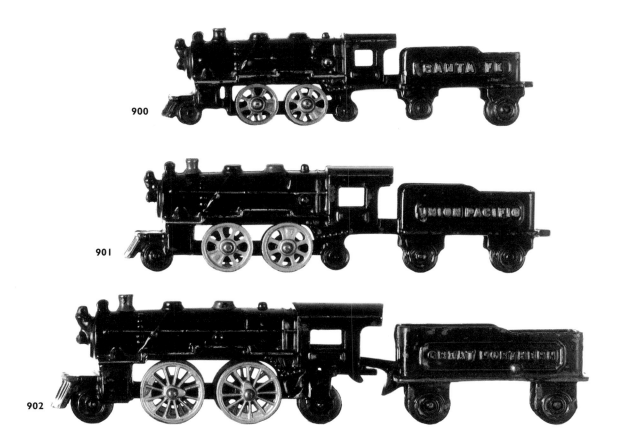

900 – KENTON
Black with gold trim, nickelplated drivers, drivers and rear tender wheels move, others are fixed. Integral tender **SANTA FE**, overall 7³/₁₆". Circa 1933. Variation: (A) similar loco with **LVRR** on tender, measuring 6¹³/₁₆" cataloged by **DENT** in 1929. (See 121, page 37)

901 – KENTON
Black with red and gold trim, nickelplated drivers, integral tender **UNION PACIFIC**, overall 8¹/₄". Circa 1933.

902 – KENTON
Black with red and gold trim, nickelplated drivers, latch couplers, loco only 6⁷/₁₆", tender **GREAT NORTHERN**. Variation: (A) green.

903 – KENTON
Black with red drivers and red trim, latch couplers, loco only 9¹/₂", tender **NYC RR CO**. Variation: (A) electro-oxidized.

920 – HUBLEY
8, only drivers move, black with gold trim and red drivers, pin couplers, 4½".

921 - HUBLEY
PRR No. 7, only drivers move, black with gold trim and nickel drivers, pin couplers, 5¾". Variation: (A) red drivers. Circa 1921-32.

922 – HUBLEY
PRR No. 6, only drivers move, latch couplers, black with gold trim and red drivers, 8¼". Circa 1921.

923 – HUBLEY
PRR No. 5, all wheels move, black with gold trim and red wheels, latch couplers, rivets above pilot, 10¹³⁄₁₆". Variation: (A) a hole in the center of the doors, probably intended for a rivet but not used. (B) rivets between the grill and the far ends of the body. Circa 1920.

Hubley electric style locomotives No. 4, 5, 6 and 7 were cataloged in 1920. The catalog illustrations show the No. 6 electric as No. 8. They do not illustrate the small No. 8 loco.

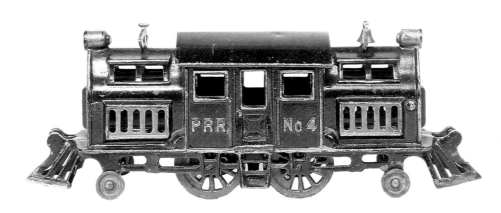

924 – HUBLEY
PRR No. 4, pressed steel roof, outboard pilot wheels, latch couplers, pantograph on one end, bell on other, ¾" diameter pilot wheels, 12³⁄₈". Variation: (A) no bell, pantographs both ends, 1" diameter pilot wheels. Cataloged in 1920 pulling **No 60 ELOISE** coaches.

950 – DENT
Attributed to DENT, **664**, 4-4-2 wheel configuration, black with gold trim, pilots and drivers are black, trailing wheels may be red or black, pilot is pierced, loco only 9⅝", eight-wheel tender **LEHIGH VALLEY**. Axles may be peened on both ends; normally round head with peen on one end.

951 – KENTON
600, 4-4-2 wheel configuration, black with red pilot and driver wheels, smokestack and top of domes; pilot is solid, loco only 9¹³/₁₆".

952 – KENTON
600, 4-4-2 wheel configuration, black with red wheels, red smokestack, pilot is pierced, loco only 9¹³/₁₆", tender **L.S.&M.S. (LAKE SHORE & MICHIGAN SOUTHERN)**. Variation: (A) solid pilot, gold trim and red paint on domes.

953 – KENTON
600, 2-6-0 wheel configuration, black with red drivers and red on smokestack and top of domes; pilot is solid, loco only 9¹³/₁₆".

954

954 – UNIDENTIFIED
A highly unusual camelback locomotive, possibly by IVES, marked **7** underneath the cab windows, 11³⁄₈".
Gertrude Hegarty Collection

Engraving from *The Railroad Gazette*, January 11, 1889

THE STRONG LOCOMOTIVE, A. G. DARWIN NO. 1.
Built by the HINKLEY LOCOMOTIVE CO., *Boston, Mass.*

LOCOMOTIVE, 4-2-0

960 – HARRIS
Black with red and gold trim; loco only 9⁷/₈"; tender **33**. This locomotive has the distinction of being the only toy loco known to have been manufactured in the 4-2-0 configuration. Variation: (A) nickelplated with tender **30**.

LOCOMOTIVES, 4-4-0

970 – COLBY
Puzzle coin bank by Edward J. Colby of Chicago, Illinois. All black except for japanned drivers. **PAT.87.** embossed under cab windows or on boiler front. Created to be a bank, a paperweight and a toy to be drawn by a child. Later versions have **SAFETY** embossed under the cab window or on the boiler front. The smokestack and second dome are held in place by a spring mechanism that is released by the weight of a full load of coins. 5¹¹/₁₆". Offered by Montgomery Ward in 1889 in nickelplated finish at 35¢ each wholesale(smokestack replaced on this piece).

971 – XL

Black with yellow wheels, yellow on dome and inside headlight and inside smokestack, bell painted gold, pilot wheels are steel, drive wheel axles are mounted in a steel frame that is bolted inside the iron casting. Pilot is a solid part of the main casting. Loco only 8 $^{15}/_{16}$". Tender shown is incorrect. It should be steel but smaller and with steel wheels, same as loco pilot wheels (see 600, page 149) and with a yellow band on upper edge. Made by PRATT & LETCHWORTH for the XL LINE OF TOYS. Loco is the same as 972 except for the wheel color. Circa 1894.

972 – BUFFALO

Black with red wheels, gold trim, red smokestack. Steel pilot wheels. Driver axles are mounted in a steel frame that's bolted inside the iron casting. Loco only 9". Tender iron with steel wheels, **870** rubberstamped in gold on black, red wheels. Pilots and pilot trucks frequently broken. Circa 1892 to 1896.

973 – WILKINS

Black, red smokestack and wheels. Separate steel bell hanger. Pilot is a separate casting. Date embossed between drivers PAT. JUNE 19.88, loco only 9$^{1}/_{16}$". Circa 1888 to 1895.

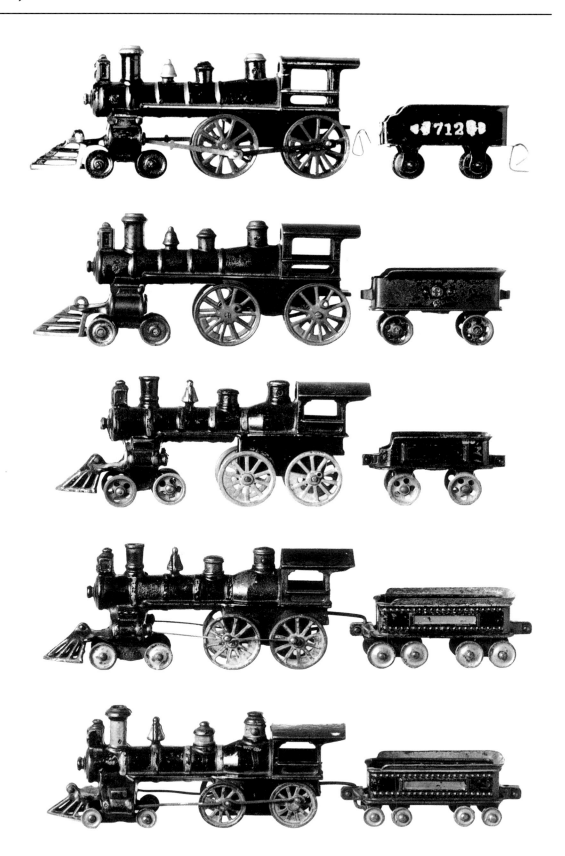

974 – HARRIS
Black with gold bands, red drivers. Original connecting rods are bare metal, the coupling rods blued, loco only 9 ³⁄₄". Steel tender **712**. The locomotive is uncataloged, but the tender appears in the 1903 HARRIS catalog with another loco. Loco is also made without connecting and coupling rods.

975 – HARRIS
Black with gold bands, red driving wheels. Made with or without connecting and coupling rods, loco only 9 ³⁄₄". Cast iron tender embossed **9**. Uncataloged, circa 1900. Variation: (A) nickel-plated.

976 – IVES
Black with gold trim, nickelplated wheels, 5-hole pilot wheels. Designed to take wire connecting rods, but never had any, loco only 9 ³⁄₈", 3 ¹⁵⁄₁₆", tall. Black tender, nickelplated 5-hole wheels, end rivets, no number.

977 – IVES
Black with gold trim, red wheels, tapered smokestack, wire connecting and coupling rods, loco only 9 ³⁄₈", 3 ¹¹⁄₁₆" tall. 8-wheel tender with **T** trucks. Variation: (A) nickelplated wheels (B) nickelplated wheels, 4-wheel tender with 5-hole wheels.

978 – IVES
Black, gold bands and bell, red trim on smokestack and domes, red wheels, connecting and coupling rods bent out of rectangular stock, loco only 9 ¹⁄₁₆", 8-wheel tender, wheels mounted in individual vertical trucks. Cataloged by IVES in 1893 and 1904.

979 – DENT
Black, gold boiler bands, pilot is solid, rear pilot wheels are cast solid; loco only 9 ³/₄", tender **999**. Variation: (A) nickelplated (B) pilot pierced, 9 ¹⁵/₁₆" (C) nickelplated.

980 – DENT
Black, gold boiler bands, also gold trim on top of rear dome, pilot and cab ridges, loco only 9 ¹¹/₁₆". Tender **P.R.R.CO.** This tender is usually with the 4-window cab loco (see 1086).

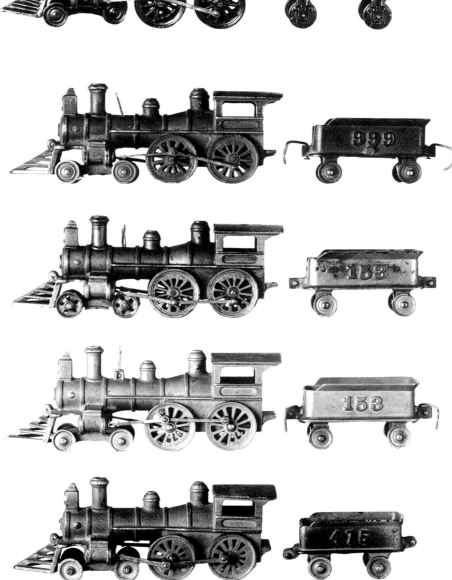

981 – IDEAL
Nickelplated, outboard solid pilot wheels, separate steel bell harp; loco only 9 ¹⁵/₁₆" to 10 ³/₁₆"; tender **999**, center rivet. Variation: (A) tender with rivets at each end in couplers (B) electro-oxidized (C) painted black with black drive wheels, gold boiler bands, axles peened on both ends, possibly made by DENT.

982 – IDEAL
Outboard five-hole pilot wheels, separate steel bell harp, nickelplated; loco only 10"; tender **153**. Circa 1895.

983 – IDEAL
Outboard solid pilot wheels, separate iron bell harp on raised mount, nickelplated; loco only 10 ³/₁₆" to 10 ¼"; tender **153**. Variation: (A) painted black with red drivers (B) nickelplated with **999** tender with center rivet (C) nickelplated with **999** tender with rivets at each end. Cataloged 1894-1910.

984 – CLIMAX
Made by COLUMBIA GREY IRON CO. outboard solid pilot wheels, made without a bell or bell harp, nickelplated; loco only 9 ¹¹/₁₆"; tender **475**. Variation: (A) black with red wheels, pilot wheels with 5 holes (B) black with red wheels, pilot wheels with 5 holes, tender **650**.

985 – ARCADE
Nickelplated, chassis has two different mounting positions for axles, wheels are presently in higher position, cast iron bell harp, loco only 9$^{15}/_{16}$", tender **808**.

986 – ARCADE
Loco same as 985, tender **1101**.

987 – IDEAL
Electro-oxidized, chassis has two positions for mounting axles which are presently in the higher position, steel bell harp, loco only 10$^{3}/_{16}$" to 10$^{1}/_{4}$", tender **999** with single center rivet. Circa 1895 to 1899, pulled nickelplated gondolas or coaches. Variation: (A) painted black with red drivers and engineer, gold trim.

988 – JONES & BIXLER
49, black, red driving wheels, outboard pilot and tender wheels, rivet at front of boiler and rear dome. Loco only 9¾", tender **49** uses a rivet in each coupler, cataloged 1909.

989 – JONES & BIXLER
49, black with red driving wheels, gold trim, inboard pilot and tender wheels, rivet at boiler front and rear dome. Loco only 9¾", tender uses a single rivet.

990 – JONES & BIXLER
49, black with red driving wheels, gold trim, single rivet in center of boiler. Loco only 9¾". Tender should be like 989.

991 – JONES & BIXLER
49, black with red driving wheels, gold trim. Thin rim driving wheels (paint restored), single rivet in the center of the boiler, inboard pilot and tender wheels. Loco only 9¾" long.

992 – HARRIS
Black, red drivers, gold trim, bell is part of the casting, no alternate axle positions, loco only 10". Tender **999**, rivets in coupler at each end. May also have come with tender **30** or **33**. Circa 1905.

993 – HARRIS
Black, red drivers, gold trim, separate cast iron bell harp, no alternate positions for axles, drive wheel diameter 55mm, loco only 10" (the same loco may have been used by ARCADE), tender **999**. Rivets in the coupler at each end. Cataloged by HARRIS in 1903 with iron coaches, 1907 with steel coaches. Variation: (A) electro-oxidized (B) painted with **712** steel tender.

994 – IDEAL
Electro-oxidized, steel bell harp, alternate positions for axles, presently in the lower holes. Driver diameter 56.5mm. Loco only 10¼", tender **999** with single center rivet. Believed to also have been sold with Ideal's larger scale 8-wheel tender marked **N.Y.C.&R.R.** Variation: (A) black, red drivers (B) copperplated (not confirmed).

995 – ATTRIBUTED TO ARCADE
Finish is mostly gone, but appears to have been painted black and probably had the normal red and gold trim. Chassis has two mounting positions for the axles, which are located in the lower position. Should have a separate bell harp. The bottom of the boiler is open the full length, which differs from the other locos in this group that have a closed belly section. Drive wheels 47.5mm diameter. Loco only 10¼". Tender **1101**. ARCADE's 1902 catalog shows this locomotive with larger drive wheels. Circa 1896 to 1905.

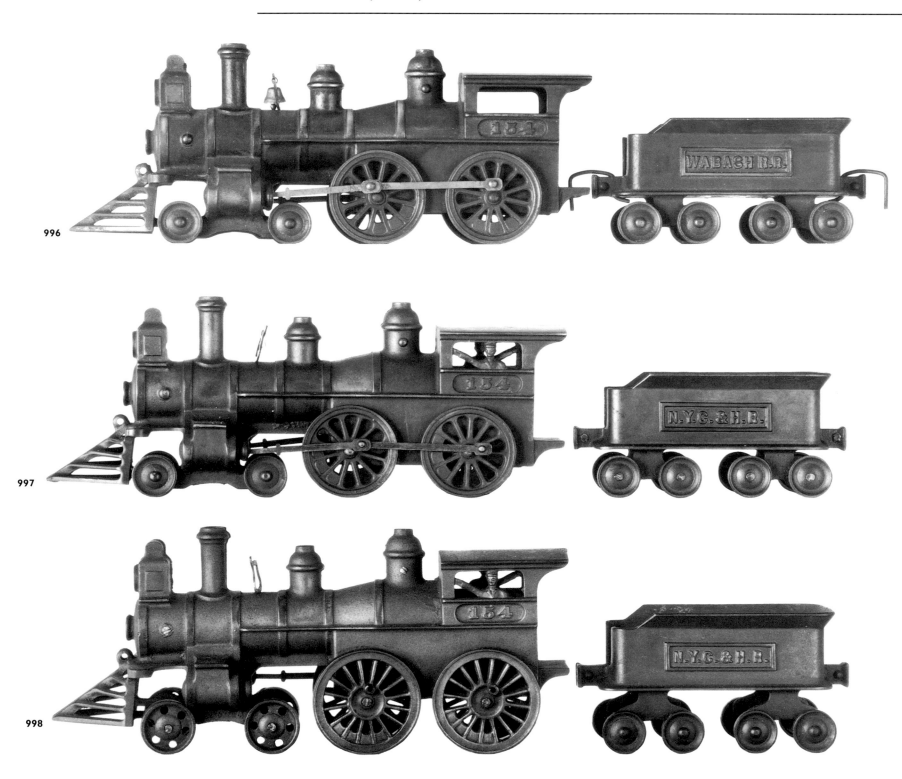

996

997

998

996 – IDEAL
154 electro-oxidized, no engineer in window, loco only 12", tender **WABASH R.R.** Variation: (A) painted black, gold trim, red orange drivers and trim.

997 – IDEAL
154, engineer in window, electro-oxidized, loco only 12", tender **N.Y.C. & H.R.** Variation: (A) painted black, red-orange drivers, gold trim.

998 – IDEAL
154 high wheel version, engineer in window, electro-oxidized, loco only 12", (missing connecting rod) tender **N.Y.C. & H.R.** Variation: (A) painted black, gold trim, red drivers, tender wheels match pilot wheels.

These electro-oxidized locomotives came with nickelplated coaches as well as coaches in a matching electro-oxidized finish. The painted locomotives came with painted coaches.

1010 – GREY IRON
60 copperplated, loco only including latch coupler 9¹⁵/₁₆", note latch coupler goes from the loco to the tender. Variation: (A) black with red and gold trim (B) nickelplated with tender **50** (C) electro-oxidized.

1011 – KENTON
Black with red and gold trim, loco only 8⁷/₈", note latch coupler goes from the tender to the loco. Cataloged by KENTON in 1914. Variation: (A) 9¹/₈", painted with pin couplers (B) 9¹/₈", nickelplated with pin couplers (C) electro-oxidized (D) nickelplated, latch couplers.

1012 – KENTON
Electro-oxidized, pin couplers, loco only 9¹/₁₆", tender **C.R.I.&P.R'Y.** (CHICAGO ROCK ISLAND & PACIFIC RAILWAY). Cataloged by KENTON in 1923.

1013 – WILKINS / KINGSBURY
Black with red and gold trim, loco only 9¹/₁₆". The casting is the same as the KENTON but slightly narrower. The pilot trucks are considerably narrower to accommodate the outboard pilot wheels which resemble HUBLEY style wheels. All axles have nail style heads instead of round rivet style, which is typical of WILKINS/KINGSBURY. A 1915 illustration shows the tender marked ERIE. In a 1911 catalog, the illustration shows the same locomotive but with the driving wheels further forward. JONES & BIXLER's 1912 catalog shows a loco with the drivers further forward and with an Ives style tin tender marked **48**. Circa 1915-1926.

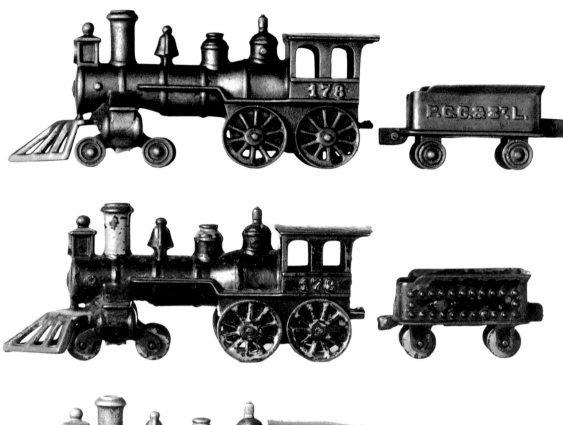

1030 – KENTON
178, finish is gone from this example but probably was painted black with the usual red wheels and gold trim; outboard pilot wheels. Loco only 8$^{15}/_{16}$". Tender **P.C.C.&ST.L.** Circa 1905.

1032 – KENTON
178, black with red wheels, red on smokestack and domes, gold trim, small diameter inboard pilot wheels, loco only 8$^{15}/_{16}$". Tender with rivet detail and inboard wheels. Variation: (A) electro-oxidized.

1033 – KENTON
178, nickelplated, large diameter inboard wheels, loco only 8$^{15}/_{16}$" Variation: (A) painted black with red wheels. Circa 1900-1912.

1034 – ATTRIBUTED TO KENTON
(possibly JONES & BIXLER) Underneath cab window is **60** (could be **80**), black with red and gold trim, 8$^{3}/_{4}$" long. Correct tender unidentified.
Hamilton Stern Collection

1035

1036

1037

1038

1039

1035 – HARRIS
Black with gold trim, red driving wheels, red on top of smoke stack and center dome; loco only 9¹¹/₁₆"; same as 1036 but with different tender.

1036 – HARRIS
Same as 1035, tender **976**. Variation: (A) nickelplated, gold trim (B) same loco with different style tender numbered **9**.

1037 – BUFFALO
Smokestack, pilot truck and pilot are three separate pieces all attached to the boiler, pilot wheels are cast iron; black with red wheels, pilot and smokestack, gold bands, cab and pilot maroon, drive wheels are mounted in normal fashion, no steel chassis, loco only 9⅞" (this example missing connecting rods and headlight finial), steel tender **870**, rubber stamped on side with **N.Y.C.&H.R.R.** near the top. Variation: (A) tender marked **123**. (B) tender marked **1**, circa 1890 to 1896. (C) Illustrated in 1890 with an eight-wheel tender **123**; no example known.

1038 – BUFFALO
Smokestack is part of the boiler casting, pilot is a separate cast iron piece, pilot truck is steel as are the pilot wheels, drivers are mounted in a steel chassis bolted to the cast iron frame; black with black cab, red wheels and smokestack, gold trim; loco only 9¾", steel tender **870 N.Y.C.&H.R.R.** lettering under lip which is usually faded away. Variation: (A) maroon cab (B) yellow wheels, sold under the XL BRAND OF TOYS (C) illustrated in 1892 with an eight-wheel tender, no example known.

1039 – BUFFALO
Smokestack is part of the boiler casting, pilot is a separate cast iron piece, pilot truck and wheels are steel, drivers are mounted in the normal fashion, no steel chassis; black with red smokestack, maroon cab and pilot, gold accents and japanned wheels; loco only 9¾", steel tender **870 N.Y.C.&H.R.R.** Circa 1890-96. Variation: (A) tender wheels red (B) iron pilot wheels like 1037, all wheels red (C) tender **1** (D) tender **123**.

1040 – XL
No markings, black with gold trim, yellow wheels and yellow on top of headlight, smokestack and domes, loco only 9¹¹/₁₆". No example of this tender is known with yellow wheels to match the loco. Made by Carpenter and sold by the XL LINE OF IRON TOYS in 1892.

1041 – CARPENTER
800 under cab window, PAT'D. JUNE 8, **80** on boiler in front of cab. Gold and red trim, red wheels, loco only 9¹¹/₁₆". Circa 1880 to 1896.

1042 – HARRIS
Black with gold boiler bands and bell, red drivers and trim, bell is a part of the casting, loco only 9⁷/₈", tender **999**, rivets at each end. Cataloged by HARRIS in 1903. Variation: (A) tender **33**.

1043 – KENTON
642, electro-oxidized, steel bell harp, loco only 9¹³/₁₆", tender **C.R.I & P.R.Y.** (CHICAGO ROCK ISLAND & PACIFIC RAILWAY). Circa 1900. Variation: (A) painted (B) painted with small tender with rivets, no lettering, inboard wheels.

EXPRESS LOCOMOTIVE, LAKE SHORE & MICHIGAN SOUTHERN.

Built by THE BROOKS LOCOMOTIVE WORKS, *Dunkirk, N. Y.*

Designed by Mr. G. W. Stevens, Supt. Motive Power.

1044 – KENTON

999, black with red wheels, gold trim, loco only 12¼", tender **N.Y.C.R.R.** pulls coaches numbered **1200** and **1201**, painted red with gold trim. Sold in 1900 with two coaches for $2.25 retail. Cataloged by KENTON in 1905.

Engraving from *The Railroad Gazette* November 16, 1888. Note similarity to the KENTON toy above.

1045 – CARPENTER

Attributed to CARPENTER; black, red wheels, gold trim. Pilot and front pilot wheels are articulated. The connecting rods are cylindrical in the manner of locomotives by BUFFALO. Drive wheels may have pie shaped counterweights. Tender unidentified. Because CARPENTER was sold to PRATT & LETCHWORTH, which sold toys under the Buffalo brand, this locomotive was likely produced by P&L, 12¼".

1046 – KENTON
999 high wheel version, 4-window cab, inboard wheels, electro-oxidized (headlight replaced), loco only 12³/₈". Tender EMPIRE STATE EXPRESS. Variation: (A) painted.

1047 – KENTON
999, 4-window cab, electro-oxidized, loco only 12¹/₄", tender EMPIRE STATE EXPRESS. Variation: (A) painted black, red wheels, gold trim. (Also see 1044, page 199.) Circa 1899.

1048 – HARRIS
6-window cab, black with red and gold trim, cast iron connecting and coupling rods, loco only 12⁹/₁₆". Tender EMPIRE STATE EXPRESS. This HARRIS tender differs from the KENTON tender above only that it's painted instead of electro-oxidized.

1049 – HARRIS
6-window cab with **B. & O.** rubber stamped in yellow underneath cab window, black with red and gold trim, cast iron connecting and coupling rods, loco only 12⁹/₁₆". Tender **917**. Locomotive is the same as 1048 except for the rubber stamped **B. & O.** Cataloged by HARRIS in 1903.

1060 – JONES & BIXLER
50, black with red drivers, gold accents, pilot wheels are japanned; loco only 10$^7/_{16}$"; did not have connecting rods, tender 49.

1061 – HUBLEY
600, black with red drivers, gold trim, pilot wheels natural iron (missing headlight); loco only 10$^{11}/_{16}$"; tender with outboard wheels P.R.R.CO. Variation: (A) nickelplated (B) large PENNSYLVANIA tender (as shown with 1090 on page 206.) Circa 1906-11.

1062 – HUBLEY
Same as 1061 but uses smaller tender with inboard wheels P.R.R. Circa 1910-11.

1063 – DENT
604, unlike 1060 through 1062, the pilot is not pierced and the second set of pilot wheels are cast solid, and there are no fender skirts over the drivers. Connecting rods missing; loco only 10$^7/_{16}$"; tender with inboard wheels P.R.R.CO.

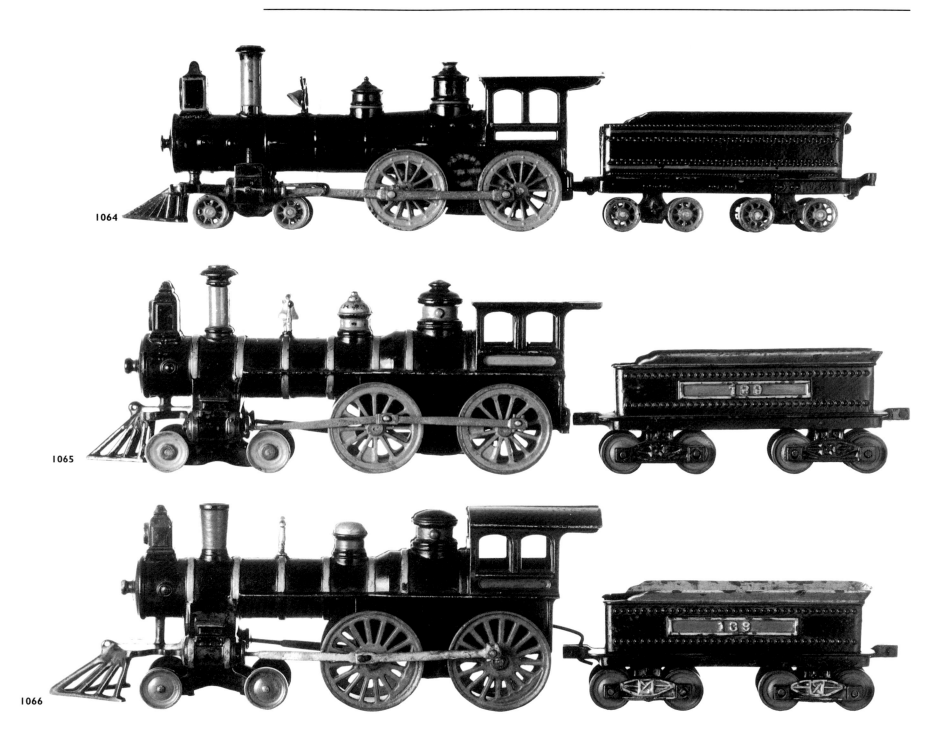

1064 – WILKINS
Black with red and gold trim, rubber stamped between drivers **PATENT APPLIED FOR** in gold, loco only 13½". Tender trucks are articulated.

Variation: (A) **PAT. JUNE 19.88** embossed in a straight line between drivers. Check closely for repairs to cab, which is frequently broken and repaired. Cataloged by WILKINS in 1895.

1065 – IVES
Black with red and gold trim, loco only 14⅝", tender **189**. Cataloged by IVES in 1893 and 1904 at $27.00 a dozen wholesale.

1066 – IVES
High wheel version, tapered smoke stack, black with red and gold trim, loco only 15¹¹/₁₆", tender **189**.

1067 – CARPENTER
870, loco only 14⅛". No cars were made to go with this big locomotive. Circa 1880.
Ward Kimball Collection

1080 – HUBLEY
Nickelplated, pin couplers, loco only
9¹/₁₆", large tender **PENNSYLVANIA**. Not
cataloged with this locomotive but
original with it.

1081 – HUBLEY
Black with gold trim, red drivers, pin
couplers, loco only 9¹/₁₆", tender **P.R.R.**
Variation: (A) nickelplated.
Circa 1914 to 1919.

1082 – HUBLEY
Painted black with nickelplated wheels,
donut style pilot wheels, latch couplers,
loco only 8¹⁵/₁₆", tender **P.R.R.**

1083 – HUBLEY
Same as 1082 but with red drivers and
regular flat pilot wheels, latch coupler,
loco only 8¹⁵/₁₆", tender **P.R.R.** Variation:
(A) nickelplated. Circa 1920 to 1932.

1084 – IVES
Catalog No. 320, black, red wheels, gold striping, silver around windows, three tin boiler bands, pilot wheels are tin (coupler pin under cab is broken off), loco only 9¹/₁₆", tin tender **L.V.E. No. 11**, pulled tin cars. Cataloged by IVES 1910 to 1912.

1085 – DENT
Black, red drivers, gold trim, silver around windows. Most cast iron locomotives have boiler bands painted gold, if painted at all, but these are painted silver to imitate the separate tin boiler bands on the similar IVES locomotives. Loco only 9¹/₈". Pin couplers, tender **999**, end rivets.

1086 – DENT
Loco same as 1085. Tender **P.R.R. Co.**

1087 – IVES (same as 1089)
Black with red wheels, silver trim around windows, roof and headlight outlined in gold and red. Three tin boiler bands, separate steel handrails and stanchions, steel bell harp (bell missing), **40** stamped on boiler front, tin pilot wheels, catalog No. 330, loco only 11³/₄". Uses a tin 8-wheel tender and pulls tin cars. Cataloged by IVES 1910 to 1912.

1088 – IVES
Black with red wheels, silver around windows, roof outlined in red and gold trim, may have had **40** stamped on boiler front, 3 tin boiler bands, steel handrails and stanchions, tin pilot wheels, bell is part of the iron casting, vertical ridges on steam chest, oval indentation under cab windows, length 11⁵/₈", came with an 8-wheel tin tender and tin cars. Cataloged by IVES 1910 to 1912.

DICK KAPLAN PHOTO

1089 – IVES *(same as 1088)*
Big sleek **40** loco, separate steel bell harp, tin tender with smooth sides. Variation: (A) tender with rivet detail and border panel embossed, green frame. This iron locomotive is scarce, the tin tender very rare. Circa 1910-12. *From a private collection*

1090 – HUBLEY
857, black, gold trim, red drivers, japanned pilot wheels, steel cab roof, steel bell harp (bell missing), loco only 11¾" long; pin couplers, tender **PENNSYLVANIA**. Variation: (A) bell part of casting. Circa 1914-19.

1091 – HUBLEY
857, black, gold trim, red drivers, natural or japanned pilot wheels, latch couplers, steel bell harp (bell missing), loco only 11½". Variation: (A) nickelplated wheels. Pilot wheels fat donut style (B) electro-oxidized. Cataloged 1920-32

The boilers, pilot, steam chest, etc., on the locomotives on this page are nearly identical to the big IVES 40 (1089, page 206). The tall windows, compared to the Ives low profile windows, are the major change. It is believed that Ives was the first one and the others copied Ives.

1092 – KENTON
Electro-oxidized, latch couplers, pilot wheels spaced same gauge width as drivers, loco only 11³/₈", 4-wheel tender, cataloged by KENTON in 1914 and 1923.

1093 – KENTON
Black with red wheels, sand dome and smokestack red, gold trim, latch couplers, pilot wheels spaced same gauge width as drivers, locomotive is the same casting as 1092. Loco only 11³/₈". 8-wheel tender. Cataloged by KENTON in 1923.

1094 – KENTON
Electro-oxidized, pin couplers, pilot wheels spaced same gauge width as drivers (example missing steel connecting rods), loco only 11³/₈", 8-wheel tender.

1095 – KENTON
(possibly JONES & BIXLER)
Black, red sand dome and smokestack, gold trim, (drivers on this example appear to be black overpainted on original red, missing steel connecting rods), pin couplers, gauge width on pilot wheels is much narrower than drivers, loco only 11⁷/₁₆". 8-wheel tender. The 1912 JONES & BIXLER catalog illustrates a comparable locomotive except with outboard pilot wheels and a tender that resembles the big IVES tin tender with 8-wheels numbered **49**.

1096 – KENTON
Black, red wheels, gold trim. Pin couplers and narrow gauge pilot wheels (example missing headlight and steel connecting rods and paint), length 11⁷/₁₆". 8-wheel tender **EMPIRE STATE EXPRESS**. Came in a set with No. 1200 NEW YORK BAGGAGE and 1201 CHICAGO PULLMAN.

1097 – GREY IRON
Electro-oxidized, latch couplers (locomotive missing coupler), narrow gauge pilot wheels, length 11¼". 8-wheel tender **70**. Variation: (A) painted black, drivers, dome and smoke stack red, gold trim. (B) cataloged with KENTON style drive wheels.

1098 – BUFFALO

BY PRATT AND LETCHWORTH
Airbrake (barrel like appendage below boiler) is a separate wood piece. Wheels, stack and domes painted red orange, gold trim, **1771** rubber stamped on cab, missing separate bronze bell harp, loco 16¼". Tender would be like 1099 but probably with red wheels to match the loco.

1099 – BUFFALO

BY PRATT AND LETCHWORTH
1771, same as 1098 except no red paint. Narrow band of gold trim around base of both domes and outlining driving wheels, missing separate bronze bell harp. Tender rubber stamped **N.Y.C. & H.R.R.R., 1771** on rear. Axles use a wire spreader to hold wheels in place. Variation: (A) loco rubber stamped **999**. Cataloged in 1892 as number **880** and the tender shown with outboard wheels. No example known.

1100 – KENTON

Barrel-shaped airbrake underneath boiler is a part of the iron casting, the pilot is made of bronze (the BUFFALO is cast iron). This example is repainted. The lettering under the cab is not correct, should be **999**, loco only 15⅞" (casting is the same length as the others. The pilot was either made a bit shorter or flattened from use. The valve is missing from the top of the rear dome.) **EMPIRE STATE EXPRESS** tender uses steel sleeves on axles to keep wheels spread.

1101 – KENTON

Electro-oxidized finish, otherwise same as 1100. Wheels and drive rods nickelplated. Note valve on top of rear dome (probably broken off from 1100, but was not made on the BUFFALO version), loco only 16¼". The original embossed lettering and rivets have been ground off the restored tender. A coil spring on each axle keeps the nickelplated wheels spread. The electro-oxidized engine and tender were cataloged in 1914 with a painted combine and coach. Circa 1905 to 1914.

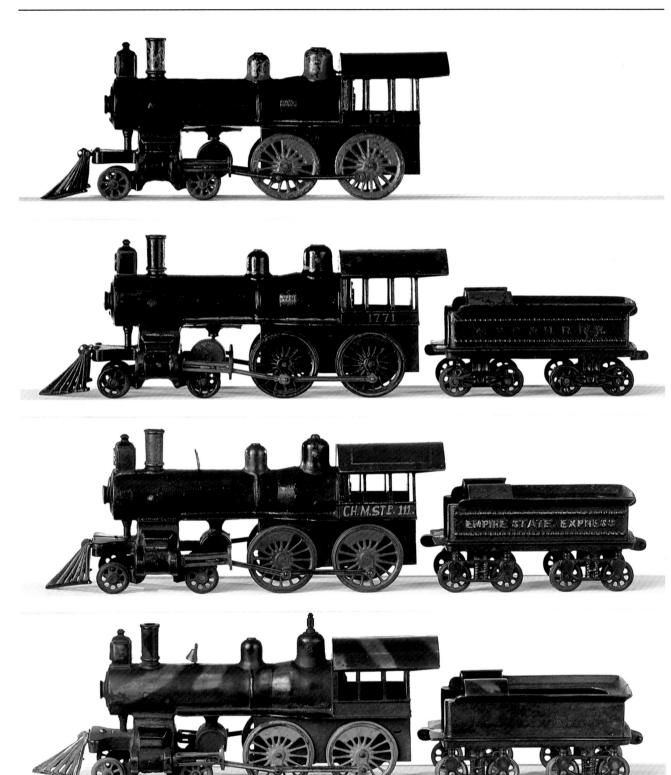

The famous engine, number 999 of the NEW YORK CENTRAL, which made a record of 118½ miles an hour, with the EMPIRE STATE EXPRESS, May 10th 1893. This is the prototype after which BUFFALO patterned its biggest toy locomotives.

Cardboard puzzle, 18" by 24", made by New York's McLoughlin Bros. in 1901, features the "999 EMPIRE STATE EXPRESS."

LOCOMOTIVE, 2-6-0

1110 – UNIDENTIFIED
Nickelplated, lacking the refinement of design detail and casting quality of most iron trains. May not be of commercial manufacture, 9³/₈". Tender unknown.

LOCOMOTIVE, 4-6-2

1111 – ARCADE
Black with nickelplated wheels. The 20TH CENTURY LIMITED Hudson style locomotive, 13" long. Tender unknown. Circa 1931.
Hamilton Stern Collection

1130 – WALLWORK
4-6-0, black with green boiler, gold trim; loco only including the hook coupler, 8⁷⁄₈".

1131 – WALLWORK
4-2-2; **1892** embossed on cab (likely the first year of manufacture). Copper colored paint with gold trim; loco only including coupler, 8³⁄₁₆". Tender **EXPRESS**. Variation: (A) orange.

1132 – WALLWORK
4-4-0, orange; loco only 8⁵⁄₈". Tender (damaged) **KING EDWARD**. Variation: (A) painted copper.

Wallwork trains all have flanged wheels but were not intended for use on tracks.

WELKER & CROSBY made trains from 1885 to approximately 1895. All locomotives have boilers and domes made of wood. The other parts are cast iron. The tenders have iron sides with a wood center. The wheels are cast iron. The pilots and front set of pilot wheels are all articulated.

1150 – WELKER & CROSBY
4-window cab. There are connecting rods from the steam chest but no coupling rods between the drive wheels (example repainted). Cab roof may be painted either black or red, 11"; uses the same tender as 1151.

1151 – WELKER & CROSBY
Same as 1150 except for the 4-4-0 wheel arrangement and coupling rods between the drive wheels. Black with red wheels, smokestack and domes, gold boiler bands; loco only 10⁷⁄₈" (lengths may vary slightly due to the position in which smokestack and steam chest assembly was nailed onto the wood boiler). Tender **W.&C.R.R.** repainted. Patented November 10, 1885.

1152 – WELKER & CROSBY
Six-window cab; black with red wheels, smokestack and domes; gold boiler bands; loco only 12¼". Tender **W.&C.R.R.** repainted.

1153 – WELKER & CROSBY
2-4-0, late model version with solid pilot wheels. Small tender with outboard wheels. Circa 1892-95.
Ed Hyers Photo

19th Century locomotive picture puzzle, 18" × 25", by McLoughlin Bros. of New York, featuring a 4-4-0 six-window cab locomotive that apparently served as a model for WELKER & CROSBY.

1170 – KENTON
Loco **100** with original red paint job.
When loco is lifted up, cogs on left side
driver engage with a protrusion on the
frame to hold the motor from running
until it is set back down. Outboard pilot
wheels; sold in 1902 for $9.00 a dozen
wholesale, 7$^7/_{16}$". Variation: 1173
(page 215).

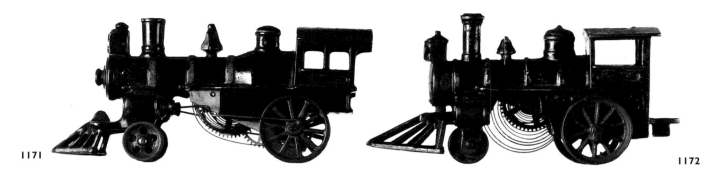

1171

1172

1171 – IVES
Black with gold trim, nickelplated wheels, clockwork motor is in a brass frame, 7¹³/₁₆". Sold with or without a tender (see 976 on page 189 for correct tender). Cataloged by IVES, circa 1903.

1172 – HUBLEY
Black with gold trim, red drivers, inboard pilot wheels, 7¹¹/₁₆". Drive wheels may be wide or narrow rim.

1173

1174

1173 – KENTON
KENTON 100, red with gold trim, black wheels, inboard pilot wheels, 7⁷/₁₆". Variation: 1170 (page 214) outboard pilot wheels.

1174 – HUBLEY
Black with gold trim, red wheels, 7⁵/₈", outboard pilot wheels. Sold by Sears for 50¢ in 1900. Cataloged by HUBLEY in 1906.

1175

1175 – ATTRIBUTED TO JONES & BIXLER
Black with gold trim, red wheels, 7⁷/₁₆".

1176

1176 – BUFFALO
Black with red smoke stack and wheels, gold trim, pilot wheels are flat steel mounted in a steel frame. The casting halves are bolted together at the boiler front and riveted in the dome. Did not have a tender, 7½". (In this example, a piece of the frame is missing from under the cab and one connecting rod is missing.)

1177

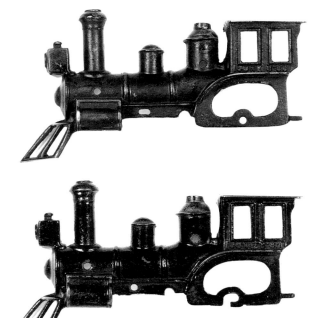

1178

These castings of the left side of two variations of the Carpenter clockwork locomotive (1177) show how, in the upper example, the main axle went through a hole in the frame. The lower casting with the notch allows the motor to be inserted and removed for servicing without removing the wheels.

1177 – CARPENTER
JUNE 8'80 embossed under cab window on left side, **PATENTED** on right side, black with gold trim and red wheels, main axle goes through a hole in the frame, 8 1/8", (wheels are replaced). Variation: (A) frame notched for main axle to allow removal of motor without removing wheels from the axle. Circa 1888-89.

1178 – SECOR
No markings, black with red and gold trim, boiler front and pilot are one separate piece, loco only 9". The floor board that protrudes beyond the cab is frequently broken off. Variation: (A) **PAT'D JUNE 8, 1880** embossed on boiler front. The retail price in 1880, $2.00.

1179 – CARPENTER
MOGUL, black with red and gold trim; probably sold without a tender, 10 1/8". Circa 1888-89.
Hamilton Stern Collection

1179

MECHANICAL IRON LOCOMOTIVES

Ives clockwork locomotive as shown in the 1885 wholesale catalog of Meinecke & Co., Milwaukee, Wisconsin.

No. 19/9.   One of the best and cheapest toys yet made. They are very strong,
                and work perfectly either in a straight line or a circle, 7 in. long. . .per doz. $9.00
No. 19/11.   9 1/2 inches long . . . .   "   16.50

1180 – IVES
Black with red and gold trim, pilot wheels are japanned. This loco most commonly bears the **PAT. AUG.19.84.** patent date under the cab window on the left side. It's unusual that this example is without that embossing. The loco also came in an unpowered model still using the same interior chassis of either brass or steel. The pilot is frequently broken off from the boiler front. Check for repairs in this area. Loco only 7", tender red with japanned wheels. Stenciled in black **U.P.R.R.,** too faint on this example to show in the photograph. Variation: (A) black tender with gold trim and gold stenciled **R.R.,** (B) **PAT. AUG.19,84** embossed under cab window. Cataloged by IVES in 1893 at $9.00 a dozen without the tender or $12.00 a dozen with the tender. The catalog illustration shows the tender with large wheels similar to those on the tender below. Circa 1884 to 1895.

1181 – IVES
PAT .AUG.19.84 embossed under the window on the left side, black with red and gold trim, loco only 9⁷/₁₆", tender **R.R.** screenprinted in gold on black, red wheels. Note front tender wheel was factory installed backwards. What appears to be curtains in the cab windows is actually excess casting material. The IVES 1893 catalog offered the locomotive without a tender at $18.00 a dozen wholesale or $21.00 with tender. The illustration showed spoke wheels on the tender. Circa 1884 to 1895.

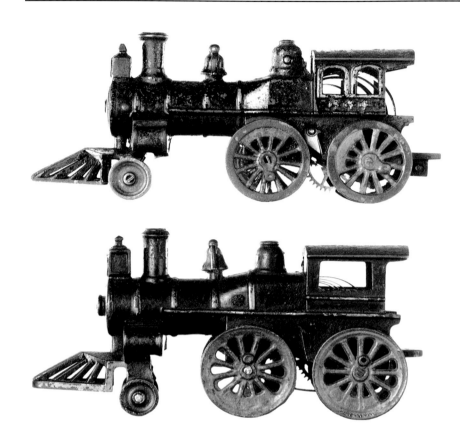

1182 – HUBLEY
444, black with red drivers, natural pilot wheels, gold trim, 9³/₈". Shown in 1906 HUBLEY catalog with drive rods.

1183 – JONES & BIXLER
Black with gold trim, red drivers, black pilots, 8¹⁵/₁₆". WILKINS cataloged a comparable locomotive in 1895. The illustration showed coupling rods, no number and small pilot wheels — typical WILKINS.

1184 – WELKER & CROSBY
The boiler, domes and tender chassis are made of wood, the rest cast iron. The pilot is articulated so the toy can be set to run in a circle. The locomotives had connecting rods only, no coupling rods to the rear wheels. The clockwork models were sold with or without a tender. If this example had been sold with a tender there would be a hole for attachment in the area protruding behind the cab. It is unusual that this roof is painted red; most are black. The tender is repainted. The tender should have solid disc wheels to be correct with this clockwork locomotive. The locomotive measures 11⁵/₈" long not including the tender. Wheels are flanged but not intended for a track. Sold in 1890 without a tender, $15 a dozen. Circa 1885 to 1890.

1185 – SECOR BRIDGEPORT
PUCK PAT'D JUNE 8 80 embossed on boiler. **FRR** embossed under cab windows. Smokestack, pilot and pilot truck are all separate attached pieces. The two halves of the main casting are bolted together. Black with red and gold trim. Loco only is 7¹/₁₆" long. *Hamilton Stern Collection*

1186 – BUFFALO
BY PRATT AND LETCHWORTH
The front pilot wheels can be turned to set the locomotive running in a circle. 9⁷/₈" long. The clockwork mechanism is located in the cab, much like the WELKER & CROSBY models and not by coincidence, as the designer Crosby went to PRATT & LETCHWORTH when he left WELKER & CROSBY.

1200 – ARCADE

PULLMAN RAILPLANE screenprinted in white on the roof, tan, casting is marked on the inside ARCADE U.S.A. 879, white rubber tires, 5$\frac{1}{16}$". Variation: (A) silver with black lettering (B) blue with white lettering (C) red with white lettering (D) pale green. Cataloged by ARCADE in 1936 as No 3790X in assorted colors: red, green, brown, blue.

1201 – ARCADE

PULLMAN RAILPLANE screenprinted in white on the roof, light green, white rubber tires, inside casting marked ARCADE U.S.A., 10". Variation: (A) silver with black lettering. Cataloged by ARCADE in 1936 as No 3830X in assorted colors: blue, green, silver.

1202 – ARCADE

PULLMAN RAILPLANE screenprinted in white on sides, red, white rubber tires, inside of casting marked ARCADE U.S.A., 8$\frac{3}{4}$". Variation: (A) tan with white lettering (B) silver with black lettering (C) light green (D) blue. Cataloged by ARCADE in 1936 as No. 3800X in assorted colors: red, green, blue, silver. This piece was also made after World War II in aluminum, painted orange with white striping and black rubber tires.

1203 – ARCADE

DELUXE EXPRESS RAILPLANE PULLMAN screenprinted in white on sides, light blue, white rubber tires, marked ARCADE 882 inside engine and center car, tail car marked 882 only, lead car 8$\frac{11}{16}$", center car 8$\frac{11}{16}$", tail car 8$\frac{13}{16}$"; came in a 4-car set (2 center cars) with a total length of 31$\frac{5}{8}$", set No. 3820X. Variation: (A) silver with black lettering. Cataloged by ARCADE in 1936 as No. 3810X with two pieces, no center section, available in blue, green or silver.

1200

1201

1202

1203

1203

1203

Horse drawn street cars gave way to
20th Century electric powered trolley
cars, providing efficient transportation
for urban commuters and simplification
for toy makers.

1220

1224

1221

1225

1222

1226

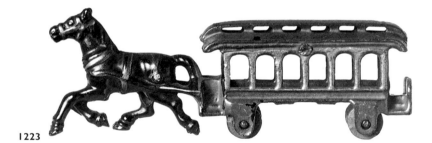

1223

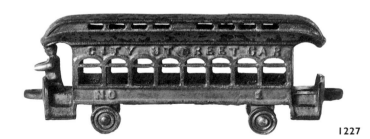

1227

1220 – HARRIS
Red, black wheels and horse with gold trim on harness and around windows, 5¹¹/₁₆". Circa 1895.

1221 – KENTON
Red with black horse, wheels may be red or silver, 6³/₈". Circa 1905-1914, cataloged by KENTON in 1914. May have been old JONES & BIXLER inventory.

1222 – CLIMAX
Attributed to CLIMAX, all silver, no moving parts, 6½".

1223 – KENTON
Attributed to KENTON, red with black horse, gold trim on harness and around windows. Appears to have first been completely painted black and then the coach overpainted red and gold trim added, 6¹¹/₁₆".

1224 – HARRIS
Red with black horse, gold trim on harness, black wheels, rubber stamped **TRANSFER** above windows. Horse is a separate piece articulated to street car (rear platform missing), 9⁵/₁₆" overall.

1225 – WILKINS
Attributed to WILKINS (possibly KENTON), red with black wheels, gold roof on clerestory, silver horses attached to a red yoke which slides into a loop on the front of the street car, 9½" overall.

1226 – KENTON
Attributed to KENTON, red with black wheels, gold highlight on lettering **TRANSFER No. 106.** Used a separate horse team and hitch similar to 1225, street car only 6½".

1227 – KENTON
Attributed to KENTON (or JONES & BIXLER), **CITY STREET CAR No. 1,** red with gold trim on windows and lettering, black wheels, nickelplated driver, used a separate horse and hitch similar to 1225, street car only 8¹/₈".

1230 – CLIMAX TOYS
Nickelplated coach and articulated yoke, horses painted gold; 9¾" overall; cataloged in 1897, painted or nickelplated version, wholesale price $33 a gross.

1231 – KENTON
Nickelplated, 10¼" overall.

1232 – UNIDENTIFIED
(possibly WILKINS)
The poor condition of this exceedingly rare streetcar makes it difficult to determine the original finish, but it's believed to have been blue with the panel below the windows painted red and rubber stamped **BROADWAY LINE** in black. The oversize black horse could be original with this piece. The car only without the horse measures 8⅝" long. Circa 1895.

1233 – HARRIS
CONSOLIDATED STREET R. 712 rubber stamped in black on all-red street car; gold trim around windows, black wheels, open floor; street car only 8³/₄", with horse (like 1234), 13¹/₂". Circa 1895-1900.

1234 – HARRIS
WORLDS FAIR STREET R.R. 372 rubber stamped in black on red body; yellow roof on clerestory, black wheels, gold trim around windows; six iron passengers—three of which are nickelplated and three painted, attached to a sheet metal floor which moves back and forth when the toy is pulled along. Driver is believed to be correct, but not confirmed. Street car only 8³/₄", with horse 13¹/₂". Retail price in 1896: 45 cents. Circa 1895-1900

1235 – WILKINS
BROADWAY CAR LINE 75 rubber stamped in black on red body; maroon roof on clerestory, blue trim around windows, black wheels, floor mostly solid (part of rear platform missing from this example). Street car only 11⁷/₈", with horse approximately 18". Sold in 1896 with two horses for 85 cents retail. Variation: (A) nickelplated car, marked BROADWAY CAR LINE 712, horse painted white. Cataloged 1896.

1236 – WILKINS
WORLDS FAIR CAR LINE 712 rubber stamped in black on red body; dark red roof, yellow roof on clerestory, blue trim around windows, black wheels, floor mostly solid; replacement driver may not be correct; pulled by two horses, overall 18¹/₂". Variation: (A) BROADWAY CAR LINE 712 with two horses. The 1895 catalog shows this street car marked WEST END STREET RAILROAD CROSS TOWN 220 with two horses or 215 with one horse.

The similarity between the small Harris street car and the large Wilkins is obviously not coincidental. It's unknown whether Harris took the liberty of copying the Wilkins cars, if permission was given or if the castings were bought from Wilkins. The use of Harris wheels and distinctive Harris four-point axle peens confirms that the Wilkins cars were indeed assembled by and presumably sold by Harris. Even when the small Harris car and the large Wilkins car use the same number, 712, the rubber stamp is different.

1237 – UNIDENTIFIED
Trolley coin bank with coin slot just below roof line. What looks like a big rivet in the center window is a turn latch to release the two halves. Japanned finish with gold trim, 4⅝".

1238 – A. C. WILLIAMS
MAIN STREET savings bank. The two halves are screwed together with a stove bolt. Painted gold, 6¹¹⁄₁₆".

1239 – SHIMER
Trolley coin bank made by Shimer,
japanned finish with gold trim, 8⅝"
long, patented March 14, 1893.
Mike Henry Collection

1240

1240B

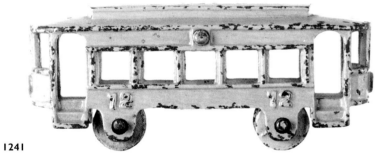

1241

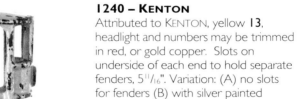

1242

1240 – KENTON

Attributed to KENTON, yellow **13**, headlight and numbers may be trimmed in red, or gold copper. Slots on underside of each end to hold separate fenders, $5^{11}/_{16}$". Variation: (A) no slots for fenders (B) with silver painted fenders. The fenders are separate insert pieces and seldom found with the trolley. Overall length with fenders $7^{1}/_{8}$".

1241 – KENTON

Attributed to KENTON, **12**, construction yellow with black numerals, gold headlights, reinforcement inside roof, $4^{15}/_{16}$". Variation: (A) pale yellow, with copper paint on numerals.

1242 – KENTON

Attributed to KENTON, yellow **12**; headlights, numerals and panel above windows painted red. Inside reinforcements in the clerestory (1241 has them in the roof area.) Slightly shorter than 1241, $4^{7}/_{8}$".

1243 – DENT
TOONERVILLE TROLLEY from the 1920s comic strip. Shown in the DENT No. 10 catalog, published about 1930. This example is one of a number of TOONERVILLE trolleys assembled from leftover castings, after the Dent Hardware Company went out of business in 1973. The box is old; unused stock found in the factory. One wheel is mounted off-center on each axle to create an erratic action as the toy is pulled along. Painted various colors.

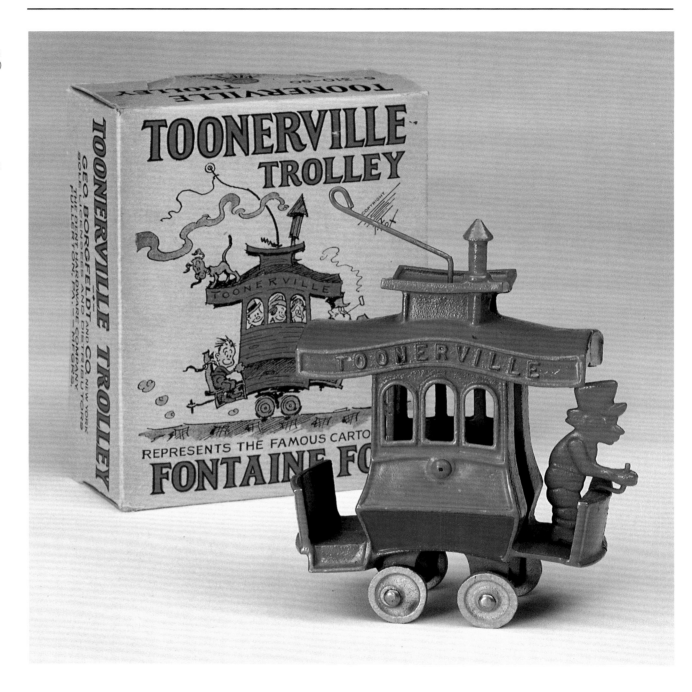

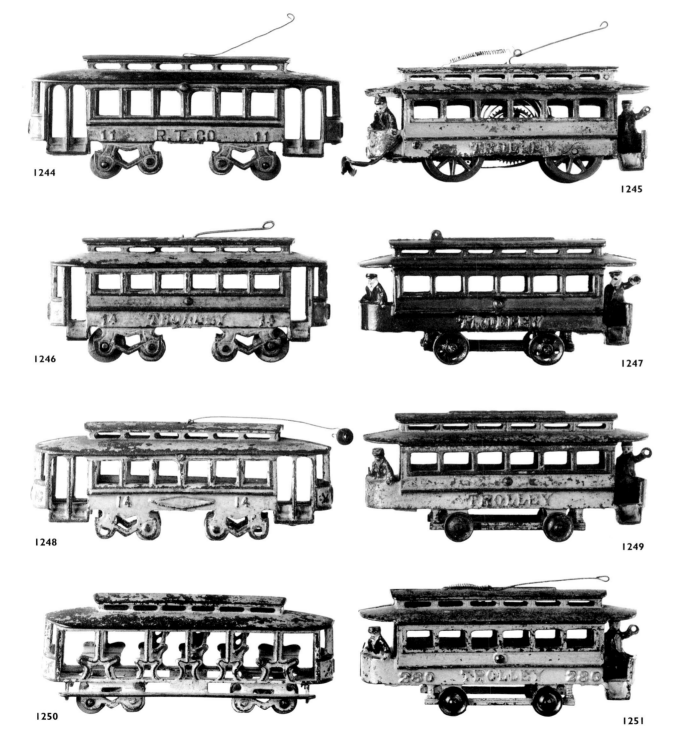

1244

1245

1246

1247

1248

1249

1250

1251

1247 and 1251 by HARRIS are virtually copies of 1249 by IVES. The 3/16" difference in length is attributed to the shrinkage factor when Harris used the IVES casting as a pattern.

1244 – KENTON
Attributed to KENTON, 11 R.T.Co., yellow, red lettering, 8⁷/₁₆". Variation: (A) green with gold lettering.

1245 – IVES
Attributed to IVES, clockwork trolley yellow, copper band above windows, red wheels, blue coats and handpainted faces on conductors; 7⁷/₈" long not counting bumper. Variation: (A) red with gold highlights, nickelplated wheels, conductors painted silver.

1246 – KENTON
TROLLEY 14 single door model, yellow with red painted in the band under the windows and highlighting the lettering, numerals and headlight, 7⁵/₈". Illustrated in a jobber catalog in 1905. (Probably originally made by JONES & BIXLER, later sold by KENTON and cataloged by KENTON in 1914 and 1927). Sold in 1900 for 25¢ retail.

1247 – HARRIS
Blue with red band under windows, gold lettering, white faces on conductors, 7³/₁₆". Variation: (A) orange with yellow band, gold letters (B) yellow, red band, black letters. Cataloged by HARRIS 1906.*

1248 – JONES & BIXLER
Attributed to J&B; may also have been sold by KENTON. 14 double door model, yellow with red numerals and headlights. (Example is missing its moveable wheels.) 8³/₁₆".

1249 – IVES
Yellow, conductors with blue coats and painted faces, 8".*

1250 – KENTON
Open air or summer trolley, white with red trim on the ends of seats and headlights, 8". Cataloged by KENTON in 1914, 1927.

1251 – HARRIS
Attributed to HARRIS; 280 trolley, yellow with cooper trim on lettering, blue jackets on conductors, japanned wheels, 7¹³/₁₆".*

1252 – KENTON
Attributed to KENTON; NATIONAL
TRANSIT CO.15, single door at each
end, yellow with red panel below
windows, gold lettering, all wheels
rotate, 12". Variation: (A) headlights and
panel under windows painted copper,
gold lettering (B) with fender inserts
(see page 231).

1253 – KENTON
Attributed to KENTON; NATIONAL
TRANSIT CO. 15, double doors at each
end, yellow with red lettering, conductor is a separate casting, 12¼". Variation: (A) yellow with red panel below
windows, lettering highlighted in gold
(B) may have been sold with fender
inserts, not confirmed.

1254 – DENT
RAPID TRANSIT CO. 15, no paint on
this example, but believed to have
been green with black wheels, 12¾".
Wheels towards the center do not
move, double doors at each end.
Circa 1907.

1252B – KENTON
Single-door 12" trolley with cast iron fender inserts at each end. The double-door 12¼" model (1253) was also made with guides on the bottom of each end to hold fender inserts. I presume most of the trolleys were sold without the separate fenders and most of the original fenders were lost, as they are extremely rare today.
Gertrude Hegarty Collection

CARS:
PASSENGER & FREIGHT

The passenger cars in this section are grouped primarily by style: first the early models with open platforms followed by the later cars with enclosed vestibules. Within these two groups, cars are arranged from the smallest 4-wheel models to the largest, then the smallest to largest 8-wheel cars, then the 12-wheel models.

Following the cast iron passenger cars are steel passenger cars, steel freight cars and tin passenger and freight cars. The steel and tin cars are included in this book because each was a component in a set sold with a cast iron locomotive.

After the tin cars, you'll find cast iron freight cars in alphabetical order by style, followed by the cabooses which, of course, bring up the rear.

On the following pages, nearly identical items made by various manufacturers are grouped together in order to make small individual differences apparent, and to facilitate identification of specific items.

"Variation" is used to indicate a second or third variety. A car with variations A and B, therefore, exists in three known types.

Preceeding pages: Down by the IVES station, early in the morning, lead passengers await departure on the ROYAL BLUE LINE cast iron coaches by the HARRIS TOY CO.

Opposite: Toy passenger coaches were painted in colors more to please a child's fancy than to replicate real railroad schemes.

1275

1270 – IVES
Black with gold trim, 3⁷/₁₆".
Circa 1889-1904.

1276

1271 – IVES
12-window, red, japanned wheels, 3⁵/₁₆".

1277

1272 – WILKINS
12-window, red, black wheels; identical
to 1271 except slightly longer and
wheels are flatter; 3⁵/₈".

1275 – UNIDENTIFIED
Possibly DENT or IDEAL; **PENNSYLVANIA
R.R.**, red-orange, gold trim, outboard
wheels, rivets in coupler at each end,
4¹⁵/₁₆".

1276 – UNIDENTIFIED
Possibly JONES & BIXLER
PENNSYLVANIA R.R. 33, red-orange,
gold trim, inboard wheels, single center
rivet, 4⁵/₁₆".

1273 – WILKINS
12-window, red, protruding couplers,
3⁵/₈". Cataloged by WILKINS, 1892-95.
Variation: (A) blue. A combine car was
also cataloged.

1277 – DENT
Attributed to DENT; **PENNSYLVANIA
R.R.**, nickelplated, rivets in couplers at
each end, inboard wheels, 4¹³/₁₆".
Variation: (A) red.

1274 – HARRIS
14-window, red, 3¹¹/₁₆".

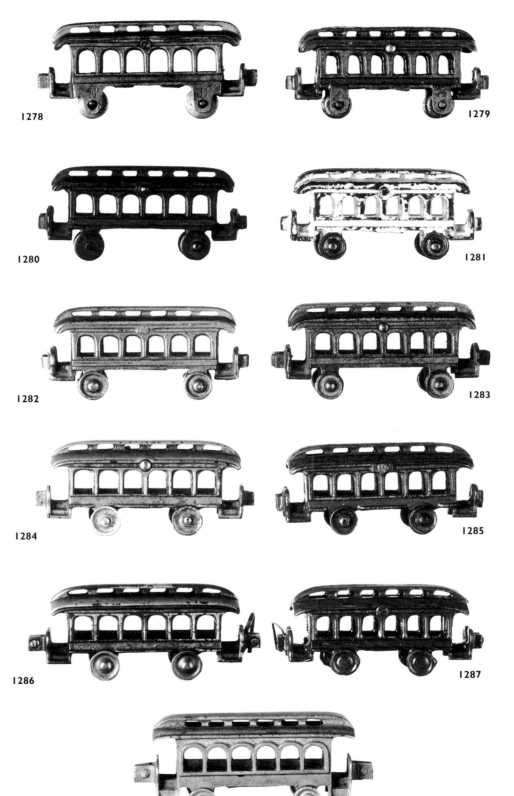

1278 – KENTON
Nickelplated, **E** stamped into each truck, 4½". Variation: (A) red.

1279 – UNIDENTIFIED
Possibly JONES & BIXLER; all red, single center rivet, 4¼".

1280 – HARRIS
Attributed to HARRIS; red, flat wheels, 4³/₁₆".

1281 – JONES & BIXLER
White with gold roof on clerestory, 4¼". Variation: (A) red (B) blue. Circa 1912.

1282 – HARRIS
Nickelplated, rounded couplers, 4⁵/₁₆". Variation: (A) red (B) white (C) blue.

1283 – HARRIS
Nickelplated, square couplers, 4⁹/₁₆". Circa 1899.

1284 – ARCADE
Also sold by Ideal; nickelplated, 4⁹/₁₆" to 4⁵/₈". Cataloged in 1902 and 1923.

1285 – CLIMAX
Red with gold trim, 4³/₈".

1286 – IDEAL
Attributed to IDEAL; nickelplated, 4⁹/₁₆".

1287 – KENTON
Attributed to KENTON; red, no moving parts, 4³/₈". Variation: (A) painted silver. Circa 1897.

1288 – ARCADE
Nickelplated, rivets in couplers at each end, 5⅛".

1289 – KENTON
Red, black wheel, single center rivet, 5¹⁵/₁₆". Variation: (A) nickelplated.

1290 – HARRIS
Nickelplated, single center rivet, outboard wheels, 6".

1291 – JONES & BIXLER
Red with gold trim around windows, black wheels, single center rivet, inboard wheels, 6". Variation: (A) green with gold around windows.

1292 – JONES & BIXLER
(Later manufactured by KENTON), green with gold trim around windows, outboard wheels, single center rivet, note raised flat area around rivet, 6". Variation: (A) yellow.

1293 – HARRIS
Red with black wheels and rivets, 6¹¹/₁₆".

1294 – HARRIS
Nickelplated, single center rivet, 6³/₁₆". Variation: (A) red with black wheels.

1295 – HARRIS
Red with darker red roof, black wheels, end rivets, 6¹/₈".

1296 – BUFFALO
Red with black steel wheels, 6¹/₁₆".

1297 – JONES & BIXLER
Attributed to JONES & BIXLER (possibly KENTON); LEHIGH VALLEY R.R. NO 7, nickelplated, 6". Variation: (A) red.

1289   1290

1291   1292

1293   1294

1295   1296

1297

1298 – CLIMAX
(Attributed to CLIMAX, possibly IDEAL or ARCADE); nickelplated, single center rivet, made with or without gussets inside the axle posts, 6$^1/_{16}$". Circa 1897. Variation: (A) painted tuscan (B) red.

1299 – ARCADE (OR IDEAL)
Red, single center rivet, 6$^3/_{16}$" to 6$^1/_4$". Variation: (A) nickelplated. Cataloged by ARCADE 1902 to 1923. Also sold by IDEAL. The IDEAL catalog, circa 1894 to 1899, shows the same coach but with rivets at each end in the coupler. There is no example available to confirm these were made. Coaches came with a 151 loco by IDEAL, which also may have been sold by ARCADE.

1300 – ARCADE
N.Y.C. & H.R.R.R., nickelplated, 7$^{15}/_{16}$".

1301 – KENTON
Attributed to KENTON; red with black wheels, floor is mostly open, 6$^{13}/_{16}$". Variation: (A) floor mostly solid with 4 oval openings. Circa 1900.

1302 – KENTON
Red, end rivets, 7$^1/_2$". Variation: (A) nickelplated 7$^9/_{16}$".

1303 – DENT
Brown with green roof on clerestory, 7$^5/_{16}$". Circa 1900 to 1907. Frequently came in a red, white and blue set. In 1907 available individually. Variation (A) red (B) white (C) blue (D) nickelplated (E) electro-oxidized (F) 7$^7/_{16}$" red-orange (G) 7$^7/_{16}$" blue (H) blue, red on clerestory roof.

1304 – ARCADE (OR IDEAL)
Nickelplated, single center rivet, 182 embossed on the insides, 7$^1/_2$". Cataloged by ARCADE in 1903 and again in 1923. Variation: (A) smaller solid wheels. An 1899 jobber catalog shows these coaches and variation (A) in IDEAL sets, indicating the coach was sold by both ARCADE and IDEAL.

1305 – KENTON
Nickelplated, end rivets, 7$^1/_2$". Variation: (A) red with gold trim, black wheels.

1306

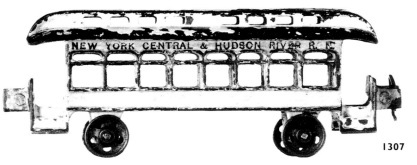

1307

1308

1309

1310

1311

1306 – IVES
WHIST PAT. APR. 30. 95, japanned with red wheels, figures painted, 8". Cataloged by IVES 1902 to 1904. Variation: (A) red.

1307 – HARRIS
NEW YORK CENTRAL & HUDSON RIVER R.R. rubberstamped in dark blue on white, wheels unfinished, 8⅝". Variation: (A) blue with gold lettering (B) red. Illustrated in an 1895 jobber catalog.   A baggage car was illustrated too.

1308 – IVES
QUEEN, japanned finish, red wheels, 8⅛".

1309 – IVES
QUEEN, green with gold trim, nickelplated wheels, 8⅞". Variation: (A) red with gold trim, nickelplated wheels.

1310 – HARRIS
NEW YORK CENTRAL & HUDSON RIVER RAIL ROAD. MAIL BAGGAGE, rubber stamped in black on red, wheels unfinished, roof maroon, 8¹³⁄₁₆". Variation: (A) **R.R.** instead of RAIL ROAD (B) nickelplated with **R.R.** instead of RAIL ROAD (C) nickelplated and rubber stamped **MICHIGAN CENTRAL RAIL ROAD CO.** Circa 1895.

1311 – HARRIS
NEW YORK CENTRAL & HUDSON RIVER RAIL ROAD., rubber stamped in black on red, wheels unfinished, roof maroon, 8¹³⁄₁₆". Variation: (A) **R.R.** instead of RAILROAD (B) nickelplated with **R.R.** instead of RAILROAD (C) nickelplated and rubber stamped **MICHIGAN CENTRAL RAIL ROAD CO.** Circa 1895.

1312

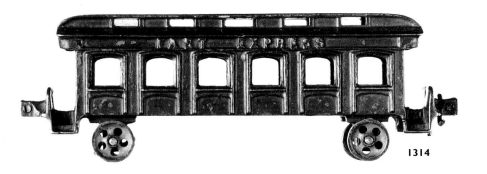

1314

1313

1315

1312 – CLIMAX
JUNIATA, 7⁷⁄₈". Cataloged by CLIMAX in 1897.

1313 – CLIMAX
P.R.R. PAYCAR, 7¹⁵⁄₁₆". Cataloged by CLIMAX in 1897.

Both 1312 and 1313 have been repainted black with gold trim and red wheels. The 1897 Columbia Grey Iron Co. catalog featuring their line of Climax toys describes the finish on these cars as "japanned and gold, red wheels." The term "japanned" generally refers to a shellac finish but, in this case, black could be the correct color scheme. A third car in this set was lettered COLUMBIA.

1314 – IVES
FAST EXPRESS, dark blue, red wheels, gold lettering, solid floor. 10⅛". Variation: (A) red, center of floor open, wheels may be black or red. Cataloged by IVES 1902-04.

1315 – STEVENS
NPR, dark brown with gold accents, platforms are slotted for separate conductors. The spindly axle posts are often broken, 9½".

1316 – CARPENTER
C.P.R.R., red. May have a separate conductor standing on the platform, attached with the coupling pin, 7⁷⁄₈". Circa 1884.

1316

1330 – WILKINS
Red with black wheels, 6³/₁₆".
Circa 1892-1903.

1331 – WILKINS
Red with black iron wheels, flathead rivet, 6¼". Variation: (A) light blue (B) dark blue (C) white. Circa 1892-1903.

1332 – BUFFALO
Red with japanned steel wheels, round head rivet, 6¹/₁₆".

1333 – IDEAL
Red-orange with yellow wheels, rivets on each end, solid cast floor, 7¹³/₁₆". Circa 1895-99. Variation: (A) nickelplated by DENT, cataloged 1894.

1334 – IDEAL
Red including wheels, rivets on each end, open bottom, 7¼". Variation: (A) nickelplated (B) red with black wheels, axles peened both ends, 7⁵/₁₆" (C) inside set of wheels are fixed, painted all red, moveable wheels were black but factory overpainted red, 7⁵/₁₆" to 7⁷/₁₆" by DENT. Circa 1894-99.

1335 – CLIMAX
Yellow with red-orange wheels, single center rivet, reinforcing ridge at center of trucks, open floor, 7¼". Variation: (A) red (B) navy blue (C) black 182 embossed inside, 7⁷/₁₆" (D) red-orange, black wheels, 7⁷/₁₆" (E) nickelplated, 7⁷/₁₆". The 7⁷/₁₆" revisions are attributed to IDEAL. Circa 1897.

1336 – CLIMAX
Nickelplated, single center rivet, open floor, flat trucks, 7¼". Variation: (A) white with red-orange wheels, 7⁷/₁₆" attributed to IDEAL.

1337 – JONES & BIXLER
Green with gold trim, wheels at each end are movable, inside wheels are cast solid, 6³/₄". Variation: (A) dark red (B) silver. Cataloged in 1909 in a set of one each, red, white and blue, pulled by a No. 55 electric style steeple cab locomotive. The coaches have no couplers and no hole or other facility for a coupler and quite frankly, I don't know how they coupled together.

1338 – JONES & BIXLER
Silver with gold trim, wheels at each end move, wheels near center are cast solid, 7³/₁₆".

1330

1331   1332

1333   1334

1335   1336

1337

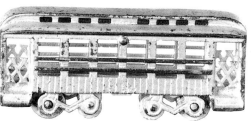
1338

1339 – WILKINS
BAGGAGE EXPRESS U.S. MAIL SMOKER, red-orange with black wheels, (example repainted), 12¹/₁₆". Variation: (A) tuscan, wheels painted red over black. Circa 1890-95.

1340 – WILKINS
Red to red-orange with black wheels, 12¹/₁₆". Variation: (A) tuscan, wheels red painted over black. Circa 1890-95.

1341 – XL (ALSO BUFFALO)
NEW YORK CENTRAL & HUDSON RIVER rubber-stamped in black on yellow body, black trim around windows, black wheels; sheet metal floor, steel wheels, 11⁵/₁₆". Variation: (A) red. The red version is believed to be BUFFALO, the yellow XL brand, both made by PRATT & LETCHWORTH. Circa 1892-96.

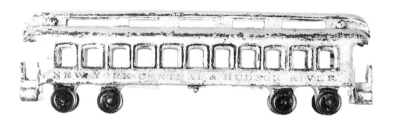

1342 – IVES
LIMITED EXPRESS 188 embossed, tuscan with red wheels, gold trim, may have some handpainted decorations in gold on the clerestory roof, small wheel version, 12½". Variation: (A) all white with red wheels. Circa 1893 to 1904.

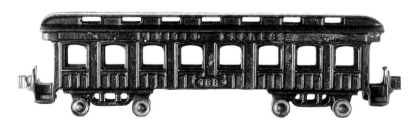

1343 – IVES
LIMITED EXPRESS 188, tuscan with red wheels, may have some handpainted decorations on the roof of the clerestory, solid floor. Larger wheel version has some casting reinforcements underneath platform on one side, generally not present on small wheel version; 12⁷/₁₆". Variation: (A) floor open down the center.

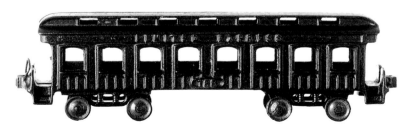

1344 – IVES
Four color variations of coaches from the PRESIDENT set. PAT. APR. 30, 95 is embossed on one side, 12⅛"
Variation: (A) red (B) green (C) silver (D) mustard brown.
Circa 1895-1904.

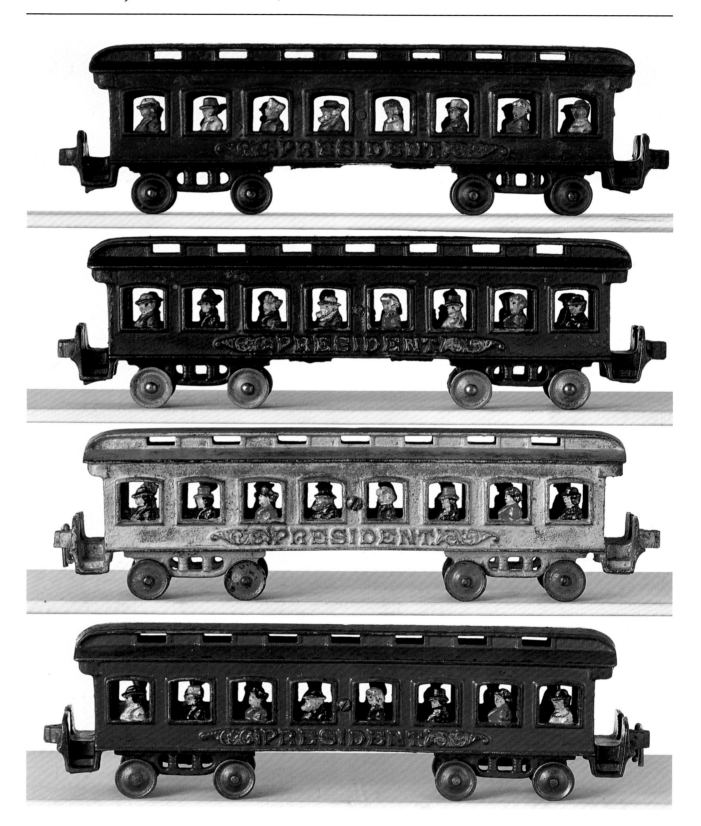

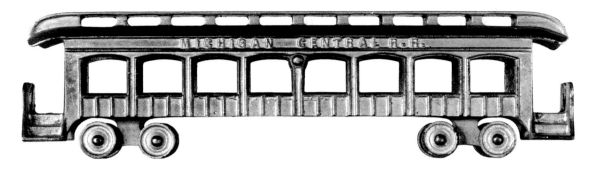

1360 – IDEAL
MICHIGAN CENTRAL R.R., nickelplated, solid floor, 13¹/₁₆". Circa 1894 to 1907.

1361 – CLIMAX
Nickelplated, no lettering, solid floor, 12¹³/₁₆". Cataloged 1897.

1362 – IDEAL
NEW YORK CENTRAL & HUDSON RIVER, nickelplated, one center rivet, solid outboard wheels, solid floor, trucks have a horizontal reinforcement ridge on inside, 13¹/₁₆". Variation: (A) no ridge inside trucks (B) reinforcement ridge inside trucks, length 12¹¹/₁₆" which is the same length as DENT.

1363 – IDEAL
NEW YORK CENTRAL & HUDSON RIVER, nickelplated, one center rivet, five-hole outboard wheels, horizontal reinforcement ridge on inside of trucks, solid floor, 13¹/₁₆". Variation: (A) open floor and PAT. PEND'G embossed vertically on right end. May have a steel floor. (Patent date refers to the iron figures attached to a sheet metal floor and moved back and forth by an axle crank. No example known.) Circa 1899.

1364 – ARCADE
CHICAGO ROCK ISLAND & PACIFIC
R.R. 52, nickelplated, single center rivet,
outboard five-hole wheels, sheet metal
floor, 12"/16". Cataloged 1902-17.

1365 – IDEAL
NEW YORK CENTRAL & HUDSON
RIVER, red body, red wheels, gold
lettering, solid outboard wheels, two
rivets, rivets and axles are peened at
both ends, solid floor, 12"/16". Variation:
(A) black wheels (B) nickelplated.

1366 – IDEAL
NEW YORK CENTRAL & HUDSON
RIVER, dark red body, gold lettering,
inside wheels are fixed, two rivets
peened on both ends, open floor,
12"/16".

1367 – DENT
NEW YORK CENTRAL & HUDSON
RIVER, inboard wheels, red-orange with
or without gold lettering, open bottom,
two rivets, 12"/16". Variation: (A) red
(B) red with blue roof on clerestory
(C) white with blue clerestory roof.
Circa 1907.

1368 – HARRIS
NEW YORK CENTRAL & HUDSON
RIVER RAIL ROAD U.S. MAIL BAGGAGE
AND EXPRESS, sans serif lettering rubber
stamped in black; nickelplated finish,
solid iron floor, 13⁷/₁₆".

1369 – HARRIS
NEW YORK CENTRAL & HUDSON
RIVER R. R. U.S. MAIL BAGGAGE AND
EXPRESS, serif lettering rubber stamped
in black; red body with gold trim
around windows, solid iron floor, roof
is a darker red, clerestory roof is brown,
13³/₈". Variation: (A) sans serif lettering
(B) red with red roof, steel floor (C) 1"
oval holes in iron floor over each truck.

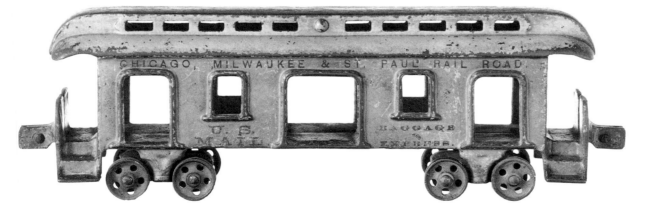

1370 – HARRIS
CHICAGO, MILWAUKEE & ST. PAUL
RAIL ROAD (sans serif), U.S. MAIL
BAGGAGE AND EXPRESS rubber
stamped in black; red body and roof
with brown roof on clerestory, gold
trim around windows, solid iron
floor, 13³/₈".

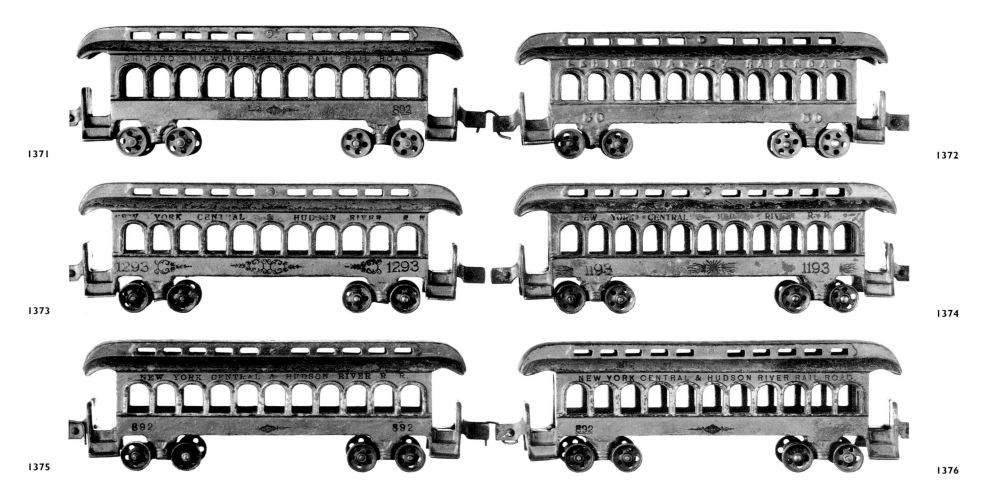

1371

1372

1373

1374

1375

1376

1371 – HARRIS
CHICAGO, MILWAUKEE & ST. PAUL RAIL ROAD. 892 sans serif lettering rubber stamped in black; red with dark brown roof on clerestory, gold trim around windows, solid cast floor, 13⁷/₁₆".

1372 – KENTON
Attributed to KENTON (possibly HARRIS); LEHIGH VALLEY RAILROAD 50 embossed; red body, darker red roof, brown roof on clerestory, lettering and windows trimmed in gold. Floor is cast iron, solid except for six ¹/₂"-diameter holes, 13".

1373 – HARRIS
NEW YORK CENTRAL & HUDSON RIVER R.R. 1293 serif lettering rubber stamped in black; all red including roof, wheels black, gold trim around the windows, steel floor, 13⁷/₁₆". Variation: (A) nickelplated, no lettering.

1374 – HARRIS
NEW YORK CENTRAL & HUDSON RIVER R.R. 1193 serif lettering rubber stamped in black; all red except roof of clerestory dark brown, black wheels; steel floor, 13⁷/₁₆". No paint left on the windows, but they were likely trimmed in gold.

1375 – HARRIS
NEW YORK CENTRAL & HUDSON RIVER R.R. 892 serif lettering rubber stamped in black; body red, roof darker red, roof of clerestory dark brown, black wheels, solid cast floor, 13⁷/₁₆".

1376 – HARRIS
NEW YORK CENTRAL & HUDSON RIVER RAIL ROAD 892 sans serif lettering rubber stamped in black; all red coach and roof, except roof of clerestory dark brown, black wheels, windows trimmed in gold, solid cast floor, 13⁷/₁₆". Variation: (A) nickelplated.

1377 – WILKINS
U.S. MAIL BAGGAGE EXPRESS combine, rubber stamped in gold, red-orange. Appears to be dipped painted after assembly since even the axles are painted. Some highlights are trimmed in gold. All trucks on the big WILKINS cars are articulated; style **B** trucks, 16⅜". Cataloged by WILKINS in 1895. Variation: (A) hand lettered **N.Y.N.H.&H.R.R.**

1378 – WILKINS
Combine U.S. MAIL EXPRESS rubber stamped in gold, gold highlights. All red-orange including axles and wheels, 16⁷⁄₁₆". Same as combine 1377 except for the style **A** trucks, which are unusual on this model.

1379 – WILKINS
LIMITED EXPRESS PARLOR CAR rubber stamped in gold, gold highlights. All red-orange including axles and wheels, style **B** trucks, 16⁵⁄₁₆". Cataloged by WILKINS in 1895.

1380 – WILKINS
LIMITED EXPRESS PARLOR CAR rubber stamped in gold, tuscan brown with red wheels, style **A** trucks. I'm not aware of a combine painted this color. 16⁵⁄₁₆". Variation: (A) red-orange. Circa 1892-95.

1381 – IVES
LIMITED VESTIBULE EXPRESS embossed, trimmed in gold, dark tuscan brown, red- orange wheels. The casting halves are bolted together instead of riveted like most iron trains. Unlike comparable WILKINS models, all with articulated trucks, each IVES truck is a solid part of the casting. In 1893 the coach was available separately; wholesale price $13.50 a dozen, 16³⁄₁₆". Variation: (A) japanned. Cataloged 1893-1904.

1382

1383

1382 – BUFFALO
Combine; transfer lettered NEW YORK CENTRAL AND HUDSON RIVER R.R. WAGNER BUFFET VESTIBULE in gold on olive body; dark brown roof on clerestory, interior and window sashes burnt orange, open platforms, 15". The 1892 catalog illustration shows outboard wheels and number **187**, though it isn't known to have been made this way.

1383 – BUFFALO
Transfer lettered NEW YORK CENTRAL AND HUDSON RIVER R.R. VANDERBILT in gold on olive body; dark brown roof on clerestory, interior and window sashes burnt orange, open platform, 20⅛". Variation: (A) same as above, without the 'R' in Vanderbilt, spelled VANDEBILT. The 1892 catalog illustration shows this coach with outboard wheels and numbered **470**, though it isn't known to have been made this way.

Kenton's versions of 1382 and 1383 are very similar, the most notable exception being Kenton's enclosed vestibules. See 1576, 1577, page 276.

1400 – KENTON
Red, 4".

1401 – KENTON
Red, 4³⁄₈".

1402 – ATTRIBUTED TO KILGORE
Red, 4⁹⁄₁₆". Variation: (A) orange.

1403 – KILGORE
Orange, 4¹⁄₁₆". Variation: (A) red.
Circa 1929 to 1931.

1404 – A. C. WILLIAMS
Blue, 4³⁄₈". Variation: (A) red.
Cataloged 1929 to 1936. Also listed
in green and tan.

1405 – KENTON
Blue, 3¹¹/₁₆". Variation: (A) white (probably came in red also).

1406 – HUBLEY
Attributed to HUBLEY; red, no moving parts, large oval holes in roof at clerestory, 3⁷/₈". Circa 1920 to 1929.

1407 – KENTON
(also JONES & BIXLER); dark red, no moving parts, 3⁷/₈" – 3¹⁵/₁₆" .

1408 – KENTON
Nickelplated, interior doorways gusseted for support, 4³/₁₆". Variation: (A) red (B) white (C) copperplated made by GREY IRON, uses an oversize rivet, 4¹/₈".

1409 – DENT
Red with blue roof on clerestory, interior doorways gusseted, 4³/₁₆". Note: diaphrams are smoother and longer than other similar coaches. Cataloged in 1914. Variation: (A) all red (B) white (C) blue (D) electro-oxidized (E) brown, green roof on clerestory (F) nickelplated.

1410 – HUBLEY
Red, no interior gussets (peen mushroomed round), 4¹/₁₆". Variation: (A) painted silver (B) nickelplated, 4¹/₈" long with no interior gussets. The shoulder line above the trucks is sloped on the HUBLEY version, squared on KENTON, (1408.)

1411 – HUBLEY
Observation, blue, 4". Variation (A) red.

1412 – GREY-IRON
Observation, orange, 4¹/₄". Cataloged in 1920.

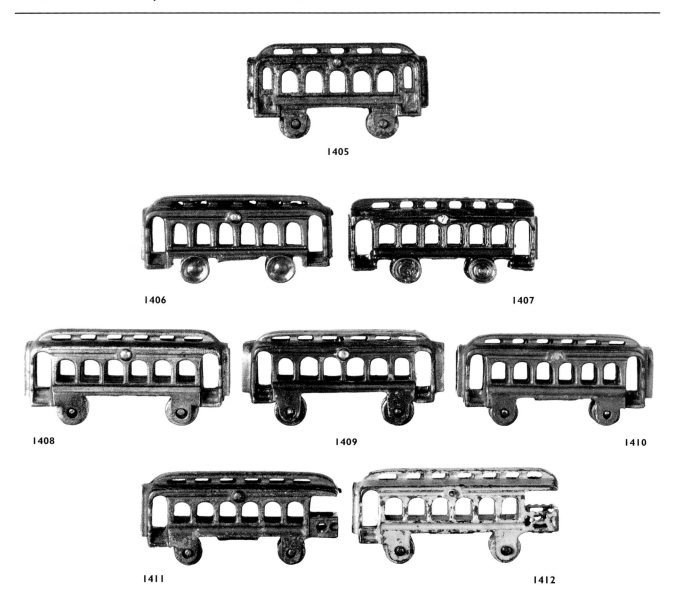

1405

1406   1407

1408   1409   1410

1411   1412

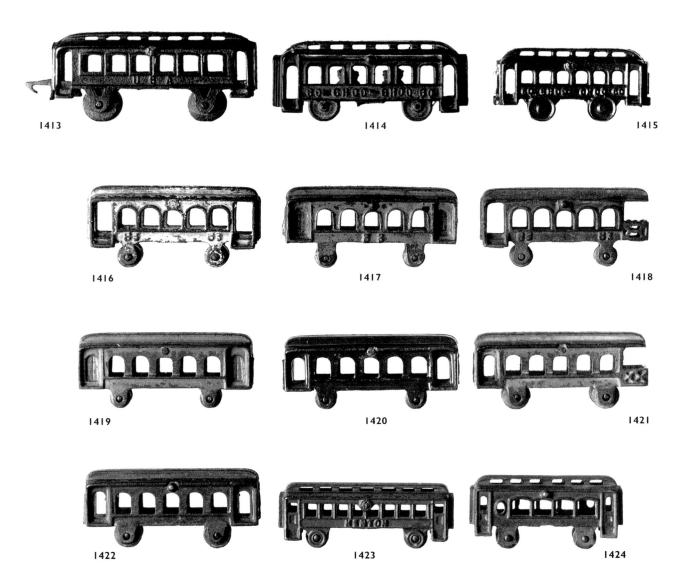

1413   1414   1415

1416   1417   1418

1419   1420   1421

1422   1423   1424

1413 – A.C. WILLIAMS
USA, red, 5⁷/₁₆" not including latch coupler. Variation: (A) black.

1414 – A.C. WILLIAMS
CHOO-CHOO 60, no moving parts, turquoise, 5¼" . Variation: (A) red (B) dark blue (C) green. Cataloged 1929.

1415 – A.C. WILLIAMS
CHOO-CHOO 60, green, 4³/₁₆" . Variation: (A) red (B) dark blue (C) turquoise. Cataloged 1929.

1416 – JONES & BIXLER
83, white, 4⁵/₈". Variation: (A) red. 1912 catalog illustration shows closed doors.

1417 – JONES & BIXLER
83, orange, 4⁵/₈''; (a similar coach with 83 on each end is illustrated in the 1914 KENTON catalog, but the artwork looks more like J&B or HARRIS).

1418 – JONES & BIXLER
83, blue. 4½".

1419 – JONES & BIXLER
Red-orange, 4¹³/₁₆". Circa 1907.

1420 – DENT*
Brown with blue clerestory, 4⁵/₈" – 4¹¹/₁₆". Variation: (A) white (B) nickelplated (C) blue (D) red.

1421 – HUBLEY
Blue, 4¹¹/₁₆". Variation: (A) orange (B) red.

1422 – HUBLEY*
Red, wheels 19mm diameter (also made with 15mm diameter wheels), 4³/₄" – 4¹³/₁₆". Variation: (A) orange (B) white (C) silver (D) blue. Cataloged 1923-32.

1423 – KENTON
Green, 4³/₄" to 4⁷/₈". Variation: (A) red (B) navy.

1424 – KENTON
Red, 4³/₁₆". Variation: (A) white.

* Coaches 1420 DENT and 1422 HUBLEY are identical except: Dent is ¹/₁₆" shorter. DENT peens are lumpy, HUBLEY's smooth; DENT axles have a lump from the casting gate, HUBLEY axles are smooth.

1425 – KENTON
Observation car, blue. 4³/₈".

1426 – KENTON
Observation car, blue. 4¹⁵/₁₆".
Cataloged 1923.

1427 – KENTON
Nickelplated, 4¹³/₁₆". Variation: (A) red.
Cataloged by KENTON in 1923.

1428 – KENTON
Green with gold trim, 6¼".
Variation: (A) navy blue (B) red.

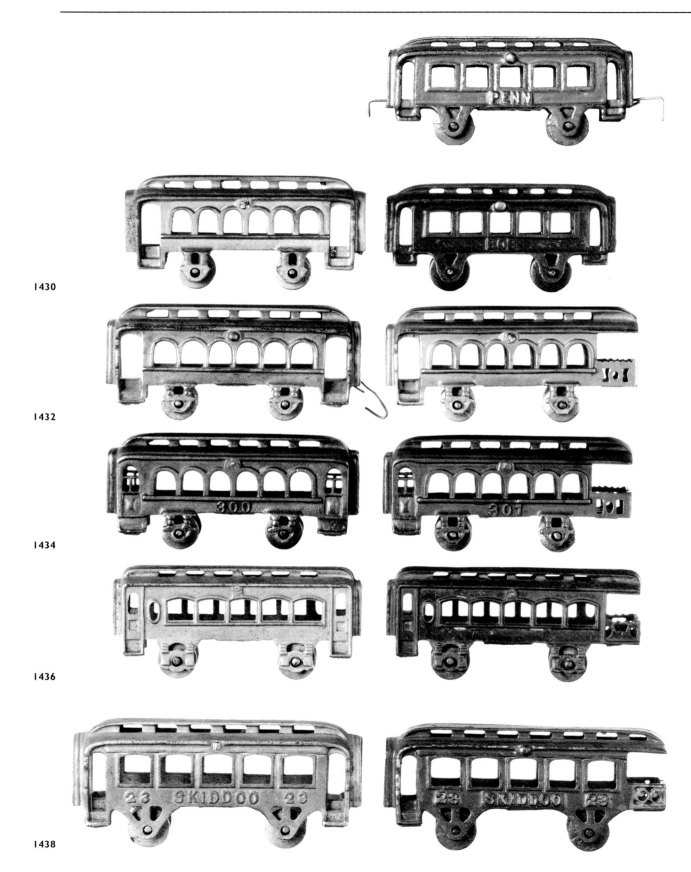

1429 – HUBLEY
PENN, red with embossed lettering highlighted in gold, 5⅝".

1430 – DENT
Nickelplated, 5½". Variation: (A) electro-oxidized (B) red with blue clerestory and gold trim (C) brown with green roof and clerestory gold trim.

1431 – DENT
Attributed to DENT (possibly HUBLEY) BOB, all red, 5¼".

1432 – KENTON
Nickelplated, 5¹¹/₁₆" to 5¹³/₁₆". Cataloged 1914.

1433 – KENTON
Nickelplated, 5¹¹/₁₆".

1434 – GREY IRON
300, copperplated, 5¹¹/₁₆". Variation: (A) nickelplated (B) red with gold trim (C) white with gold trim.

1435 – GREY IRON
301, copperplated, 5⅝". Variation: (A) nickelplated (B) blue with gold trim.

1436 – KENTON
Nickelplated, 5⅝". Variation: (A) red (B) white.

1437 – KENTON
Blue, 5¾". Variation: (A) nickelplated.

1438 – HUBLEY
23 SKIDDOO, nickelplated, 6½". Variation: (A) red (B) white (C) olive (D) silver. Sold individually in 1921. Circa 1910-28.

1439 – HUBLEY
23 SKIDDOO, red with gold trim, 6½". Variation: (A) blue (B) olive. Circa 1922-28.

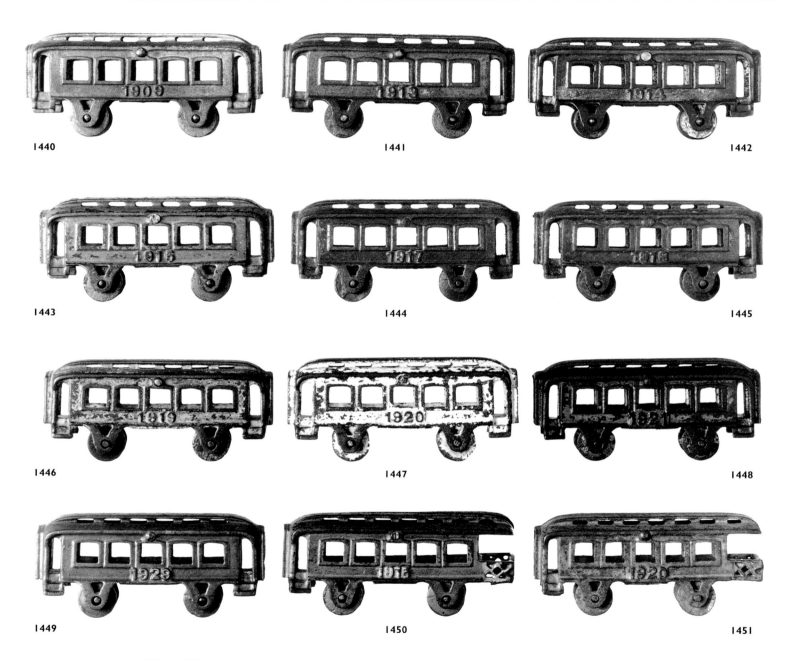

1440

1441

1442

1443

1444

1445

1446

1447

1448

1449

1450

1451

1440 – 1451 VINTAGE HUBLEYS
For each year, from at least 1909 to 1924, HUBLEY offered a set of three cars all dated for the current year. These generally came out during the holidays in the previous year and may have been sold well into the following year, depending upon inventory levels.

They were most commonly found in a set of one each red, white and blue. The 1909 and 1914 in this selection came nickelplated. Each coach and observation measured from 5⁵/₈" to 5¹¹/₁₆" long. Variation: 1445 (A) longer at 5⁷/₈" with 12 windows instead of 10, only one example seen: **1918**, red. Can't confirm maker, but resembles other HUBLEYs.

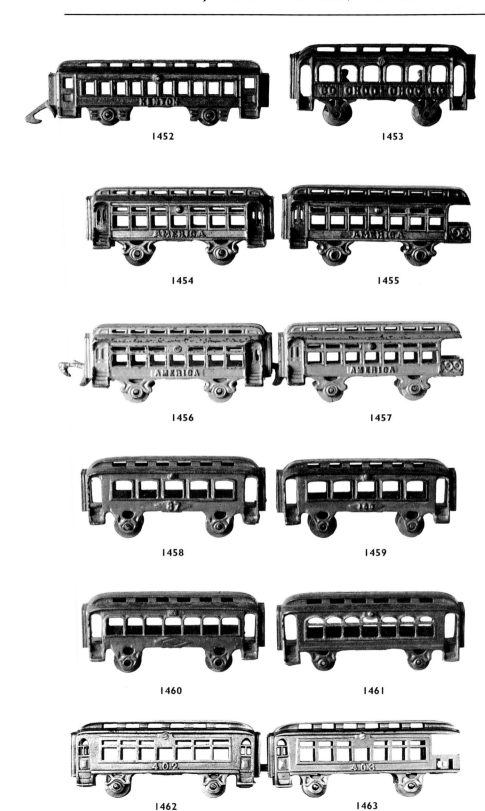

1452
1453
1454
1455
1456
1457
1458
1459
1460
1461
1462
1463

1452 – KENTON
Latch coupler, red with gold trim; 7^3/$_4$" to 7^7/$_8$" not including coupler. Variation: (A) green with gold trim (B) navy.

1453 – A.C. WILLIAMS
CHOO-CHOO 60, red, 6-1/2". Variation: (A) turquoise (B) turquoise with gold highlights (C) silver (D) blue. Cataloged about 1914 as painted "aluminum" at 84¢ a dozen wholesale. Circa 1914.

1454 – HUBLEY
AMERICA, copperplated, pin couplers, 6^5/$_8$". Circa 1914-19.

1455 – HUBLEY
AMERICA in serif letters, copperplated, pin couplers, 6^5/$_8$". Circa 1914-19.

1456 – HUBLEY
AMERICA in sans serif letters, orange, latch coupler, 6^5/$_8$" not including coupler. Variation: (A) white (B) white with serif letters (C) red with sans serif letters (D) red serif letters. Circa 1920-32.

1457 – HUBLEY
AMERICA in sans serif letters, orange with gold accents, latch coupler, 6^9/$_{16}$" not including coupler. Variation: (A) blue (B) blue with serif letters (C) copperplated with serif letters. Circa 1920-32.

1458 – JONES & BIXLER*
87, red; 6^9/$_{16}$". Variation: (A) silver. Circa 1905-09.

1459 – JONES & BIXLER*
163 red; 6^7/$_{16}$". Variation: (A) silver.

1460 – JONES & BIXLER*
Red; 6^9/$_{16}$" – 6^5/$_8$". Variation: (A) blue (B) white, blue roof on clerestory, gold trim.

1461 – KENTON
Blue with gold trim around windows, 6^3/$_4$". Variation: (A) red (B) white (C) electro-oxidized (D) nickelplated. Circa 1911-23.

1462 – GREY IRON
402, nickelplated, 6^5/$_8$" not including latch coupler. Variation: (A) electro-oxidized. May have also been finished in white or red.

1463 – GREY IRON
403, nickelplated observation car, 6^3/$_4$". Variation: (A) painted blue with gold trim. Also probably came with an electro-oxidized finish.

*1458, 1459 and 1460 were cataloged by JONES & BIXLER in 1909. The 1914 KENTON catalog also shows these coaches, probably excess from the defunct J & B Co.

1462 and 1463 were reproduced from 1947-1983 by DONSCO under the John Wright brand using the original GREY IRON patterns. The postwar versions can be identified by their rough, sandy texture and thin coat of orange paint. They are often intentionally rusted to look old. (See 455, page 131.)

1464 – HUBLEY

PENNSYLVANIA R.R. CO. NORMANDIE 333, copperplated, latch coupler, 7³⁄₈" not including coupler. Cataloged in 1920 as painted blue, but no example known. Cataloged in 1915 with pin couplers, nickelplated or painted blue or red; no example known.

1465 – HUBLEY

PENNSYLVANIA R.R. CO. NORMANDIE 333, red-orange with gold trim around windows, center rivets top and bottom, outboard wheels, pin couplers, 7⁹⁄₁₆". Cataloged by HUBLEY in 1906.

1466 – HUBLEY

PENNSYLVANIA R.R. CO. NORMANDIE 333, blue with gold trim, latch coupler, 7¹⁄₂" long not including coupler. Variation: (A) red (B) white (C) apple green (D) nickelplated (E) copperplated. Circa 1920-32.

1467 – HUBLEY

PENNSYLVANIA R.R. CO. NORMANDIE 333, blue with gold trim, center rivets top and bottom (example missing inboard wheels), pin couplers, 7⁵⁄₈". Variation: (A) red-orange with gold trim.

1468 – HUBLEY

PENNSYLVANIA R.R. CO. NORMANDIE 333, blue with gold trim, pin couplers, 7⁵⁄₈". Variation: (A) red (B) white (C) nickelplated. Circa 1915-19.

1469 – DENT

Attributed to DENT; PENNSYLVANIA R.R. CO. IVANHOE 411, red, outboard wheels, rivets in center at top and bottom, pin couplers, 7⁷⁄₁₆". Variation: (A) nickelplated.

1470 – DENT

PENNSYLVANIA R.R. CO. IVANHOE. 411, brown with gold trim, green roof on clerestory, 7¹⁄₈" to 7³⁄₁₆". Variation: (A) blue with gold trim (B) white (C) red (D) nickelplated (E) electro-oxidized (F) orange, gold trim. Cataloged 1907.

1471 – IDEAL

Attributed to IDEAL, ribbed sides, red, gold highlights around windows, yellow wheels, 182 embossed inside both sides. It's unusual for a ribbed side model, which normally has open platforms, to have the later style enclosed vestibules with diaphrams, 7¹⁄₂".

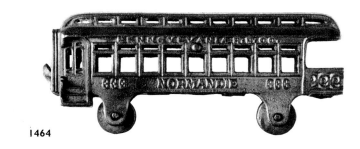

1464

1465

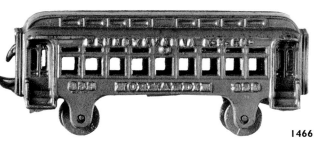

1466

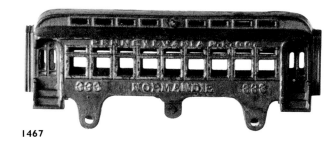

1467

1468

1469

1470

1471

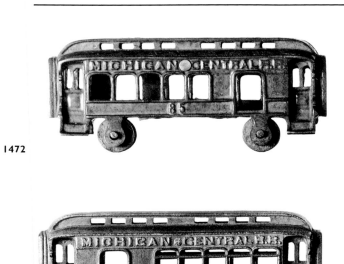

1472

1473

1474

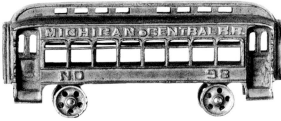

1475

1476

1477

1478

1479

1480

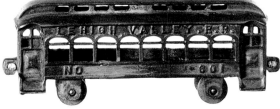

1481

1472 – JONES & BIXLER
Attributed to JONES & BIXLER, MICHIGAN CENTRAL R.R. 85, blue. Both sides of this car are the same casting; there's no left or right side; 7 7/8". Circa 1910-11.

1473 – JONES & BIXLER
Attributed to JONES & BIXLER, MICHIGAN CENTRAL R.R. No 86, red, 7 15/16". Cataloged by JONES & BIXLER, 1905-09, illustrated with outboard wheels.

1474 – HARRIS
MICHIGAN CENTRAL R.R. 68, nickel-plated, 8 1/16". A similar combine numbered 86, with solid wheels, was cataloged by JONES & BIXLER. Variation: (A) red.

1475 – HARRIS
MICHIGAN CENTRAL R.R. No 98, nickelplated, 8 1/16". Variation: (A) blue with gold trim (B) red (C) white.

1476 – ARCADE
C.R.I.&P.R.R. SMOKER 375, nickelplated, sheet metal floor, 7 15/16". Circa 1902-23.

1477 – KENTON
PENNSYLVANIA LINES 1410, electro-oxidized, 7 13/16". Variation: (A) red.

1478 – KENTON
PENNSYLVANIA LINES 1410, electro-oxidized, 8 3/16". Circa 1905. Variation: (A) red.

1479 – KENTON
PENNSYLVANIA LINES. No 1412, electro-oxidized, 8 3/16". Circa 1905. Variation: (A) red.

1480 – KENTON
LEHIGH VALLEY R.R. 9167, red, 8". Wheels are incorrect; should be outboard as in 1478.

1481 – KENTON
LEHIGH VALLEY R.R. No 801, red, 8". Wheels are incorrect; should be outboard as in 1479.

1482 – KENTON
3 ERIE RAILROAD 4, nickelplated, latch coupler, 8³/₈" not including coupler. Cataloged by KENTON, 1914-23.

1483 – KENTON
PENNSYLVANIA LINES, electro-oxidized, latch coupler, 9¹⁵/₁₆" not including coupler. Variation: (A) nickelplated. Cataloged by KENTON in 1923.

1484 – KENTON
3 ERIE RAILROAD 4, nickelplated, latch coupler, 8⁷/₁₆" not including coupler. Variation: (A) white (B) red. Cataloged by KENTON, 1914-23.

1485 – KENTON
PENNSYLVANIA LINES ROUIN, electro-oxidized, latch coupler, 9³/₈" not including coupler. Variation: (A) nickelplated. Cataloged by KENTON in 1923.

1486 – KENTON
3 ERIE RAILROAD 4, nickelplated, latch coupler, 8½" not including coupler. Variation: (A) pin couplers, red. Cataloged by KENTON, 1914-23.

1487 – KENTON
PENNSYLVANIA LINES ROUIN, nickelplated, latch coupler, 9½" not including coupler. Variation: (A) blue with gold trim, (B) electro-oxidized. Cataloged by KENTON in 1923.

1488– KENTON
SANTA FE RAILROAD GRANAGUE, nickelplated, latch coupler, 8" not including coupler. Variation: (A) red with gold trim, blue roof on clerestory (B) white with blue roof on clerestory (C) all red. Cataloged by KENTON in 1923.

1489 – KENTON
SANTA FE RAILROAD GRANAGUE, nickelplated, latch coupler, 8⅛" not including coupler. Variation: (A) blue. Cataloged by KENTON in 1923.

1482   1483

1484   1485

1486   1487

1488   1489

1490   1491

1490 – KENTON
ERIE RAILROAD PONCELOT, red with gold trim on windows, latch coupler, 6¹¹/₁₆" not including coupler. Variation: (A) white (B) electro-oxidized (C) nickelplated. Cataloged by KENTON in 1923.

1491 – KENTON
ERIE RAILROAD PONCELOT, electro-oxidized, latch coupler, 7⅛" not including coupler. Variation: (A) blue (B) nickelplated. Cataloged by KENTON in 1923.

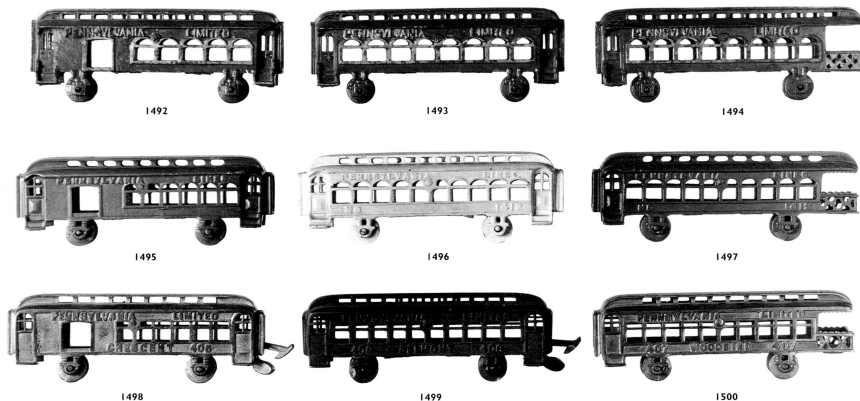

1492 1493 1494

1495 1496 1497

1498 1499 1500

1492 – DENT
PENNSYLVANIA LIMITED, combine, brown with gold trim, green roof on clerestory, pin couplers, 8^{15}/$_{16}$". Variation: (A) red with gold trim.

1493 – DENT
PENNSYLVANIA LIMITED, brown with gold trim, green roof on clerestory, pin couplers, 8^{15}/$_{16}$". Variation: (A) white with gold trim. (Reproduction of this is 8^3/$_4$", sandy texture, heavier weight.)

1494 – DENT
PENNSYLVANIA LIMITED, observation, brown with gold trim, green roof on clerestory, pin coupler, 9^3/$_8$". Variation: (A) blue with gold trim.

1495 – KENTON
PENNSYLVANIA LINES, combine, nickelplated, pin couplers, 9^1/$_{16}$". Variation: (A) electro-oxidized (B) red.

1496 – KENTON
PENNSYLVANIA LINES No 1412 nickelplated, 9^3/$_8$". Variation: (A) electro-oxidized (B) white.

1497 – KENTON
PENNSYLVANIA LINES No 1412 observation, pin coupler, nickelplated, 9^3/$_8$". Variation: (A) electro-oxidized (B) blue.

1498 – GREY IRON
PENNSYLVANIA LIMITED CRESCENT 405, combine, copperplated, bulbous weight on latch coupler, 9^1/$_{16}$" not counting coupler. Variation: (A) electro-oxidized (B) nickelplated (C) red. Also made without the bulbous coupler weight.

1499 – GREY IRON
PENNSYLVANIA LIMITED BELMONT 406, coach, electro-oxidized, bulbous weight on latch coupler, 8^7/$_8$" not including coupler. Variation: (A) copperplated (B) nickelplated (C) white. Also made without the bulbous coupler weight.

1500 – GREY IRON
PENNSYLVANIA LIMITED WOODBINE 407, observation, copperplated, latch coupler, 9^1/$_8$". Variation: (A) electro-oxidized (B) nickelplated (C) blue.

1501 – IDEAL
NEW YORK CENTRAL & HUDSON R.R. PAT. PEND'G. 1086, nickelplated; four cast iron figures attached to sheet metal floor, which moves back and forth via wire attached to crank on one axle (this example missing two figures); pin couplers, 9⁹/₁₆". Variation: (A) no figures, plain sheet metal floor (B) no figures, plain sheet metal floor, painted maroon, yellow wheels, gold roof on clerestory (C) with figures, painted maroon, yellow wheels, gold roof on clerestory.

1502 – IDEAL
NEW YORK CENTRAL & HUDSON R.R. 1086, (no patent date) nickelplated, sheet metal floor, pin couplers, 9⁵/₈" to 9¹¹/₁₆". Variation: (A) maroon, yellow wheels, gold roof on clerestory (B) all red-orange (C) nickelplated with solid wheels.

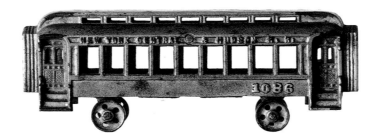

1503 – ARCADE
SAPPHO 125, nickelplated, sheet metal floor, 9⁵/₁₆". Variation: (A) red with gold trim. Circa 1902.

1504 – KENTON
PENNSYLVANIA LINE. 1410, electro-oxidized combine car, 7¹³/₁₆".

1505 – KENTON
PENNSYLVANIA LINES. NO. 1412, electro-oxidized, 9¹/₁₆''. Variation: (A) red.

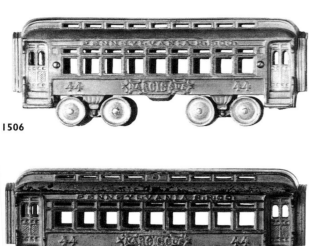

1506

1507

1508

1509

1510

1511

1512

1513

1506 – UNIDENTIFIED

Possibly IDEAL; PENNSYLVANIA R.R.CO. NARCISSUS **44**, nickel-plated, outboard wheels, two end rivets by doors, solid floor other than 6 circular holes, pin couplers, 9⁷/₁₆". (This coach, bearing the number **88**, was cataloged by JONES & BIXLER in 1909. In 1914 it was in the KENTON catalog, presumably excess from the defunct J&B.)

1507 – UNIDENTIFIED

Possibly WILKINS; NARCISSUS (no numbers), red-orange, gold trim, black wheels, steel floor, single center rivet with the WILKINS style flathead, pin couplers, 9⁵/₁₆". Variation: (A) solid wheels, 9⁷/₁₆".

1508 – HUBLEY

PENNSYLVANIA R.R. CO. NARCISSUS **44**, red-orange with gold trim, center rivet at top and bottom, outboard wheels, pin couplers, may come with or without sheet metal floor, 9⁵/₈". Cataloged by HUBLEY in 1906.

1509 – JONES & BIXLER

88, all blue with gold trim, pin couplers, single center rivet, 9⁷/₁₆". Variation: (A) red (B) yellow.

1510 – HUBLEY

PENNSYLVANIA R.R. CO. NARCISSUS **44**, red with gold trim, center rivet at top and bottom, inboard wheels, pin couplers. 9⁵/₈"

1511 – HUBLEY

PENNSYLVANIA R.R. CO. WASHING-TON **44**, nickelplated, single center rivet, inboard wheels, latch coupler, 9¹/₂" not including coupler. Goes in set with NARCISSUS observation car. Variation: (A) turquoise (B) olive (C) red (D) royal blue (E) white. Circa 1920-32.

1512 – HUBLEY

PENNSYLVANIA R.R. CO. NARCISSUS **44**, blue with gold trim, inboard wheels, single center rivet, pin couplers, 9¹¹/₁₆". Variation: (A) red (B) white (C) nickelplated. Circa 1910-19.

1513 – HUBLEY

PENNSYLVANIA R.R. CO. NARCISSUS **44**, observation nickelplated, single center rivet, inboard wheels, latch couplers, 9⁷/₁₆"-9⁹/₁₆" not including coupler. Variation: (A) olive (B) blue (C) turquoise. Illustrated from 1914 to 1919 with pin couplers (no example seen). Circa 1920-32.

1514

1515

1516

1517

1518

1519

1514 – KENTON
LAKE SHORE & MICHIGAN SOUTHERN, maroon with red-orange wheels and roof on clerestory, gold trim around windows and striping on roof, pin couplers, outboard wheels, 10¼". Variation: (A) red body, wheels and roof on clerestory red-orange (B) nickelplated. Circa 1895-1900.

1515 – KENTON
LAKE SHORE & MICHIGAN SOUTHERN, dark red with red-orange roof on clerestory, gold trim around windows on trucks and striping on roof, inboard wheels, trucks are flat without reinforcements, pin couplers. 10⅛". Circa 1900-1914.

1516 – KENTON
LAKE SHORE & MICHIGAN SOUTHERN, nickelplated, vestibules with diaphrams, pin couplers, large diameter wheels, 10⅝" to 10¹¹⁄₁₆". Variation: (A) tan with red clerestory (B) bright copperplate (C) dark red with red-orange roof on clerestory. Circa 1900-1914.

1516.1 – KENTON
Observation nickelplated (not shown), 10¹³⁄₁₆". Cataloged 1914.

1517 – KENTON
LAKE SHORE & MICHIGAN SOUTHERN, maroon with dark red roof on clerestory, gold trim around windows on trucks and striping on roof. Trucks have a reinforcing ridge not present in 1512. Pin couplers, 10¼". Variation: (A) electro-oxidized. Circa 1910 to 1914.

1518 – GREY IRON
OVERLAND LIMITED IONIC 506, sheet metal roof, red with gold trim and a latch coupler, not including coupler, 10³⁄₁₆". Variation: (A) white (B) nickelplated (C) electro-oxidized (D) copperplated.

1519 – GREY IRON
OVERLAND LIMITED DORIC 507, sheet metal roof, medium blue with gold trim, connects with a latch coupler, but since it's the last car it doesn't have a coupler, 10⅛". Variation: (A) nickelplated (B) copperplated (C) electro-oxidized.

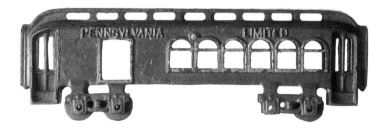

1520 – DENT
PENNSYLVANIA LIMITED, red with gold trim, blue clerestory roof, pin couplers, 11⅞".

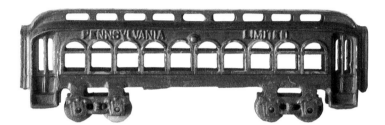

1521 – DENT
PENNSYLVANIA LIMITED, red with gold trim, blue clerestory roof, pin couplers, 12". Variation: (A) white.

1522 – DENT
PENNSYLVANIA LIMITED, all blue with gold trim, pin couplers, 12¼".

1523 – KENTON
LAKE SHORE AND MICHIGAN SOUTHERN U.S. MAIL, red with black trucks, gold lettering, dark blue clerestory roof, latch coupler; 10⅝" not including coupler. Variation: (A) electro-oxidized (B) grey with red roof. Cataloged by KENTON in 1923.

1524 – KENTON
LAKE SHORE AND MICHIGAN SOUTHERN BONVOYAGE, white, black trucks, gold lettering, blue clerestory roof, latch coupler; 10⅞" not including coupler. Variation: (A) electro-oxidized (B) grey with red roof (C) nickelplated 11". Cataloged by KENTON in 1923.

1525 – KENTON
LAKE SHORE AND MICHIGAN SOUTHERN BONVOYAGE, all blue with black trucks, gold lettering, latch coupler; 11⅛" not including coupler. Variation: (A) grey with red roof (B) nickelplated 11³⁄₁₆". Cataloged by KENTON in 1923.

1526 – KENTON
CHICAGO ROCK ISLAND AND PACIFIC U.S. MAIL, electro-oxidized, latch coupler; 11¹⁵/₁₆" not including coupler. Variation: (A) red with gold trim, blue roof. Cataloged by KENTON in 1923.

1527 – KENTON
CHICAGO ROCK ISLAND AND PACIFIC ROSITA, electro-oxidized, latch coupler; 12³/₁₆" not including coupler. Variation: (A) white with gold trim, blue roof. Cataloged by KENTON in 1923 described as a red, green and blue set.

1528 – KENTON
CHICAGO ROCK ISLAND AND PACIFIC VANDOR, electro-oxidized, latch coupler; 12½" not including coupler. Variation: (A) blue with gold trim. Cataloged by KENTON in 1923.

1529 – KENTON
NEW YORK CENTRAL, electro-oxidized, latch coupler; 11⅞" not including coupler. Variation: (A) red with black trucks (B) nickelplated.

1530 – KENTON
NEW YORK CENTRAL ROSITA, electro-oxidized, latch coupler; 11⅞" not including coupler. Variation: (A) red with black trucks (B) nickelplated.

1531

1532

1533

1534

1535

1536

1537

1538

1531 – HUBLEY
PENNSYLVANIA R.R.CO. 60 ELOISE 60, red with gold lettering, rivets at top and bottom center, pin couplers, 12³/₁₆". Variation: (A) orange (B) nickelplated. Cataloged by HUBLEY in 1906. This ELOISE car with number 90 was illustrated in the 1909 to 1912 JONES & BIXLER catalog, no example known.

1532 – JONES & BIXLER
90, rivets top and bottom center, pin coupler, blue, gold wheels, 11¹³/₁₆". Variation: (A) red. The JONES & BIXLER

1909 to 1912 catalog shows this number **90** coach with name ELOISE, no example known.

1533 – HUBLEY
PENNSYLVANIA R.R.CO. 60 ELOISE 60, latch coupler, rivets top and bottom center, red-orange, 12³/₁₆" not including coupler. Variation: (A) dark red (B) white.

1534 – JONES & BIXLER
90, blue with gold trim, inboard wheels, pin couplers, 8³/₄" opening for steel

floor, 11⁷/₈". Variation: (A) no steel floor, 10³/₄" bottom opening.

1535 – HUBLEY
PENNSYLVANIA R.R.CO. 60 ELOISE 60, red with gold trim, latch couplers, rivet at each end above windows, 11¹⁵/₁₆" not including coupler. Variation: (A) white (B) electro-oxidized. Circa 1920 to 1932.

1536 – JONES & BIXLER
92, all yellow, inboard wheels, pin couplers, 12¹³/₁₆".

1537 – HUBLEY
PENNSYLVANIA R.R.CO. 60 ELOISE 60, observation, blue, latch couplers, rivets at each end of windows, 12¹/₈" not including coupler. Circa 1920 to 1932.

1538 HUBLEY
PENNSYLVANIA R.R.CO. 60 ELOISE 60, observation, blue with gold trim, latch couplers, rivets at top and bottom center, 12⁵/₁₆" not including coupler.

1539   1540
1541   1542
1543   1544

1539 – KENTON
CHICAGO ROCK ISLAND & PACIFIC. U.S. MAIL. 1018, nickelplated, outboard wheels, protruding couplers, cast iron floor, 12^7/$_{16}$". Variation: (A) electro-oxidized (B) burnt orange body, black roof with gold edge, red roof on clerestory.

1540 – KENTON
CHICAGO ROCK ISLAND & PACIFIC. 1020, electro-oxidized, outboard wheels, protruding couplers, solid cast iron floor, 12½". Variation: (A) nickelplated (B) blue, red roof with dark brown roof on clerestory.

1541 – KENTON
CHICAGO ROCK ISLAND & PACIFIC. U.S. MAIL. 1018, nickelplated, small diameter inboard wheels (missing all but one pair), protruding couplers, sheet metal floor, 12^7/$_{16}$". Cataloged in 1910. Variation: (A) electro-oxidized (B) blue.

1542 – KENTON
CHICAGO ROCK ISLAND & PACIFIC. 1020, electro-oxidized, inboard wheels, protruding couplers, sheet metal floor, 12½". Variation: (A) nickelplated (B) blue.

1543 – KENTON
CHICAGO ROCK ISLAND & PACIFIC. U.S. MAIL. 1018, electro-oxidized, inboard wheels, vestibules with diaphrams, sheet metal floor, pin couplers, 11^{15}/$_{16}$". Circa 1900 to 1914. Variation: (A) dark blue, red roof on clerestory, gold trim.

1544 – KENTON
CHICAGO ROCK ISLAND & PACIFIC. 1020, electro-oxidized, inboard wheels, vestibules with diaphrams, sheet metal floor, pin couplers, 12^1/$_8$". Circa 1900 to 1914. Variation: (A) dark blue, red roof on clerestory, gold trim.

1545 – GREY IRON
KEYSTONE EXPRESS U.S. MAIL. CELTIC **604**, combine, electro-oxidized, bulbous weight on latch coupler (coupler broken off), 11¹⁵⁄₁₆" not including coupler. Also made without the bulbous coupler weight.

1546 – GREY IRON
KEYSTONE EXPRESS IVANHOE **605**, electro-oxidized, normal latch coupler, 11⁷⁄₈" not including coupler. Also made with bulbous coupler weight.

1547 – GREY IRON
KEYSTONE EXPRESS HYPATIA **606**, electro-oxidized, connects with latch coupler, 12⁷⁄₁₆".

1548 – DENT
Attributed to DENT; LEHIGH VALLEY BLACK DIAMOND EXPRESS CAFE CAR, japanned, silver lettering, red flag, 12⁵⁄₁₆". Variation: (A) brown with gold trim, blue roof on clerestory.

1549 – DENT
Attributed to DENT; LEHIGH VALLEY, japanned, silver lettering, red flag. 12⁷⁄₁₆". Variation: (A) may have been made in brown with blue roof.

1550 – DENT
Attributed to DENT, PULLMAN, japanned, silver lettering, red flag, gold trim on observation platform, 12⁵⁄₁₆". Variation: (A) brown with gold trim, blue roof on clerestory.

1551 – DENT

NEW YORK CENTRAL & HUDSON RIVER, all blue with gold trim on letters, ribbed sides, open floor, 12½". Variation: (A) red-orange. This unusual coach with enclosed vestibules was found in a set with the common open platform coaches, one red, one white.

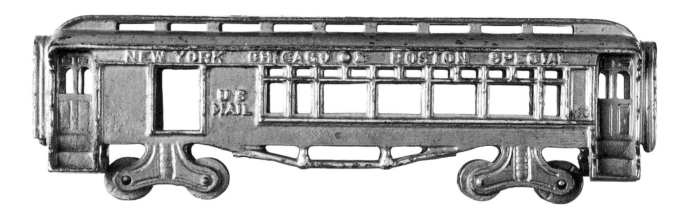

1552 – DENT

Attributed to DENT, NEW YORK CHICAGO & BOSTON SPECIAL U.S. MAIL combine, royal blue with gold trim, red roof on clerestory. Only one set of wheels on each truck move, 13¹⁄₁₆". Variation: (A) brown with gold trim, blue roof on clerestory.

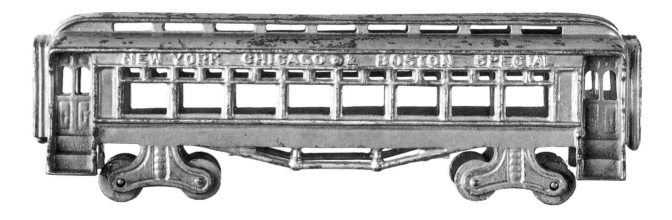

1553 – DENT

Attributed to DENT, NEW YORK CHICAGO & BOSTON SPECIAL, royal blue with gold trim and red roof on clerestory, 12¹³⁄₁₆". Only one set of wheels on each truck move.

1554

1555

1556

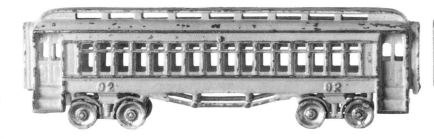

1557

1558

1559

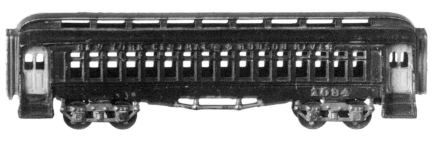

1560

1554 – WILKINS
Attributed to WILKINS, CHICAGO LIMITED rubber stamped in red, **903** embossed, yellow, red roof on clerestory, black wheels, axles peened on both ends, 14³/₈".

1555 – HARRIS
LAKE SHORE & MICHIGAN SOUTHERN U.S. MAIL BAGGAGE 1293 rubber stamped in black on red, gold trim, black wheels, 13⁷/₁₆". Variation: (A) electro-oxidized with no lettering (B) probably came in blue, rubber stamped NEW YORK CHICAGO & BOSTON LIMITED.

1556 – HARRIS
NEW YORK CHICAGO & BOSTON LIMITED 1293 rubber stamped in black on blue, gold trim, 13¼". Variation: (A) rubber stamped LAKE SHORE & MICHIGAN SOUTHERN 1293 in black on red.

1557 – JONES & BIXLER
Embossed 92, yellow with gold trim on windows and wheels, 12⁷/₈". Variation: (A) green (B) red-orange. Cataloged by JONES & BIXLER in 1912.

1558 – HARRIS
Electro-oxidized, no markings, 13³/₁₆" to 13¼".

1559 – IDEAL
NEW YORK CENTRAL & HUDSON RIVER BAGGAGE CAR 1074 SMOKING, painted tuscan with gold trim, gold on roof, yellow doors, solid wheels are incorrect, 13⁷/₁₆". Variation: (A) nickelplated (B) electro-oxidized (C) red-orange, yellow doors, gold on clerestory roof, trucks and lettering. Circa 1896 to 1903.

1560 – IDEAL
NEW YORK CENTRAL & HUDSON RIVER 1084, painted tuscan with gold trim, gold on roof and vestibule diaphrams, yellow doors. Wheels are 5-hole type mounted inboard on special axles, 13⁹/₁₆". Variation: (A) nickelplated (B) electro-oxidized (C) red-orange, yellow doors, gold trucks and trim. Circa 1896 to 1903.

1561 – IDEAL
WABASH RAILWAY-BANNER LIMITED BAGGAGE AND SMOKING CAR W.R.R., nickelplated, trucks do not have alternate axle mounting positions (this example is missing one baggage door and the nut in the center is not original), 15⁷/₁₆". Variation: (A) painted maroon with gold trim, yellow wheels (B) red with gold trim, yellow wheels.

1562 – IDEAL
WABASH RAILROAD-BANNER LIMITED, nickelplated, trucks do not have alternate axle mounting positions, floor is solid cast-iron, 15⁹/₁₆". Variation: (A) painted maroon with yellow wheels, gold trim (B) red with gold trim, yellow wheels. Circa 1895.

1563 – IDEAL
NEW YORK CENTRAL & HUDSON RIVER BAGGAGE AND SMOKING CAR W.R.R., nickelplated. Trucks have alternate axle mounting positions (so larger wheels could be used), 15³/₈". Variation: (A) electro-oxidized, (B) tuscan color, gold trim, yellow doors and wheels (C) tuscan color, gold trim, yellow doors, red wheels.

1564 – IDEAL
NEW YORK CENTRAL & HUDSON RIVER. On right end, next to door: PAT. PEND-G. Nickelplated, sheet metal floor, trucks have alternate axle mounting positions (so larger wheels could be used). This is the casting used with animated people: see 1567, page 273., 15⁹/₁₆". Variation: (A) electro-oxidized (B) painted tuscan with yellow doors and wheels, gold trim.

1565 – IDEAL
NEW YORK CENTRAL & HUDSON RIVER BAGGAGE AND SMOKING CAR, electro-oxidized. Trucks do not have alternate axle positions, 15³/₈". Variation: (A) trucks have alternate axle mounting positions and larger 33mm six-hole wheels with axles in the lower position (see page 273) (B) nickelplated (C) painted tuscan, gold trim, yellow doors and wheels, alternate axle positions, steel floor. An 1899 jobber catalog lists the finish as "blackened nickel".

1566 – IDEAL
NEW YORK CENTRAL & HUDSON RIVER., nickelplated, trucks do not have alternate axle mounting positions; solid cast iron floor. An 1899 jobber catalog lists the finish as "blackened nickel.", 15⁹/₁₆". Variation: (A) painted red-orange with yellow doors and wheels. Gold lettering and gold on diaphrams and roof on clerestory (B) electro-oxidized.

1565A – IDEAL
NEW YORK CENTRAL & HUDSON
RIVER BAGGAGE AND SMOKING CAR,
high wheel version, 15¹¹/₁₆". Trucks have two mounting positions for the axles. This example has no remaining finish. It may have originally been either nickelplated or electro-oxidized.

1567 – IDEAL
NEW YORK CENTRAL & HUDSON
RIVER, large wheel version with animated people. Cast iron figures are attached to a steel floor that shifts to and fro via a wire rod connected from the floor to an axle crank. This example has been repainted, original finish probably nickelplated, 15³/₈".
Hamilton Stem Collection

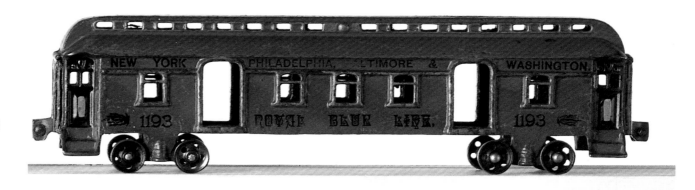

1568 – HARRIS
NEW YORK PHILADELPHIA, BALTIMORE & WASHINGTON ROYAL BLUE LINE 1193, blue-grey with red roof, dark red roof on clerestory. Gold trim around windows, ROYAL BLUE LINE in fancy lettering, solid floor, 16⅝".

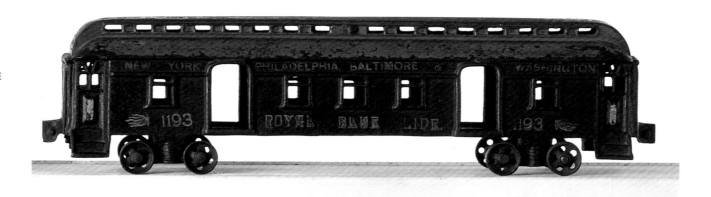

1569 – HARRIS
NEW YORK PHILADELPHIA, BALTIMORE & WASHINGTON. ROYAL BLUE LINE 1193, rubber stamped in yellow lettering, dark blue body, red orange roof, maroon roof on clerestory, ROYAL BLUE LINE in fancy lettering, solid floor, 16⅝". Variation: (A) sheet metal floor, (B) lettered in gold paint.

1570 – HARRIS
NEW YORK PHILADELPHIA, BALTIMORE & WASHINGTON ROYAL BLUE LINE 1193, rubber stamped in yellow, dark blue background, red roof, maroon roof on clerestory, ROYAL BLUE LINE in simple serif lettering, solid floor, 16⅝".

1571 – HARRIS
NEW YORK PHILADELPHIA, BALTIMORE & WASHINGTON ROYAL BLUE LINE 1193, rubber stamped in black on mustard body, brown roof, red roof on clerestory, solid floor, 16⅝". Cataloged 1903.

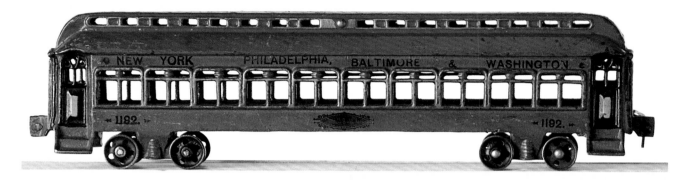

1572 – HARRIS
NEW YORK PHILADELPHIA, BALTIMORE & WASHINGTON 1192 rubber stamped on blue-grey body, red roof, dark red roof on clerestory, gold trim around windows, 1192 in small numbers, solid floor, 16¾".

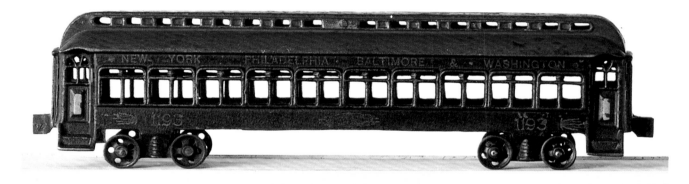

1573 – HARRIS
NEW YORK PHILADELPHIA, BALTIMORE & WASHINGTON 1193 rubber stamped in yellow, dark blue body, red roof, maroon roof on clerestory, 16¾". Variation: (A) lettering in gold paint with small 1192 on one side only, no numbers on the other side, red-orange roof, maroon roof on clerestory.

1574 – HARRIS
NEW YORK CHICAGO & BOSTON SPECIAL 1193 rubber stamped in black, all red-orange body, gold trim around windows and clerestory windows, solid floors, 16¾". Variation: (A) blue.

1575 – HARRIS
NEW YORK PHILADELPHIA, BALTIMORE & WASHINGTON 1193 rubber stamped in black on mustard body, brown roof, red roof on clerestory, solid floor, 16¾". Cataloged 1903.

1576

1577

1576 – KENTON

Combine; lettered in gold on green, interior and window sashes burnt orange, roof on clerestory black (example restored), 15¼". Variation: (A) black trucks, dark red roof on clerestory with gold striping.

1577 – KENTON

Lettered in gold on green, interior and window sashes burnt orange, roof on clerestory black (example restored), 20⁷⁄₁₆". Variation: (A) black trucks, dark red roof on clerestory with gold striping. Cataloged 1905.

NOTE: Coaches quite similar to 1576 and 1577 were sold under the Buffalo brand, the most notable difference being the open platforms on the Buffalo models instead of Kenton's enclosed vestibules. (See 1377, 1378, page 250.)

1590 – KENTON
NEW YORK CENTRAL AND HUDSON
RIVER R.R. BAGGAGE, red, blue roof,
red roof on clerestory, gold trim, black
trucks, large diameter wheels (some
wheels missing on this example), uses
four wheels on each six-wheel style
truck, latch coupler, steel floor, 15³⁄₈".
Circa 1923.

1591 – KENTON
NEW YORK CENTRAL AND HUDSON
RIVER BAGGAGE NEW YORK 1200,
electro-oxidized, solid floor, tall
couplers, outboard wheels, center set
of wheels on each truck fixed, 16¼"

1592 – KENTON
NEW YORK AND CHICAGO LIMITED
BAGGAGE 1200, solid floor, red with
gold trim, outboard wheels black,
center set of wheels on each truck
fixed, short couplers, 16¹³⁄₁₆". Variation:
(A) tall couplers. Circa 1900.

1593 – KENTON
NEW YORK CENTRAL AND HUDSON
RIVER BAGGAGE NEW YORK 1200, red
body, black trucks, blue roof, dark red
clerestory roof with gold striping, sheet
metal floor, tall couplers, large diameter
wheels, 12-wheel style trucks use only
eight wheels, 16¼". Variation: (A)
electro-oxidized (B) electro-oxidized
but with smaller diameter wheels
(C) red-orange body, blue roof, dark
red roof on clerestory, small diameter
wheels. Cataloged by KENTON in 1914.

1594 – GREY IRON
BROADWAY LIMITED BAGGAGE
OVERBROOK 704, electro-oxidized,
sheet metal floor, latch coupler,
15½" to 15⁵⁄₈" not including coupler,
12-wheel style trucks actually use eight
wheels. Variation: (A) painted red, gold
trim. Cataloged 1920.

1595 – KENTON
NEW YORK CENTRAL & HUDSON RIVER R.R. MAGNOLIA red with blue roof, red roof on clerestory, gold trim, latch couplers; 15⁹⁄₁₆" not counting coupler. Twelve-wheel style trucks actually use eight wheels (wheels on this example are incorrect; should be larger diameter as in 1598). Cataloged by KENTON 1923.

1596 – KENTON
NEW YORK AND CHICAGO LIMITED 1201, red with gold trim, black wheels (example missing some wheels), 16⅛". Circa 1900.

1597 – KENTON
NEW YORK CENTRAL & HUDSON RIVER CHICAGO 1201 electro-oxidized; 12 wheels, but center wheels on each truck are cast solid; pin couplers (example missing some wheels), 16³⁄₁₆".

1598 – KENTON
NEW YORK CENTRAL & HUDSON RIVER CHICAGO 1201 electro-oxidized; 12-wheel style only uses eight inboard wheels; pin couplers, 16³⁄₁₆". Variation: (A) red-orange, blue roof, dark red on clerestory with small wheels, gold striping on clerestory (B) electro-oxidized with small wheels. Cataloged by KENTON in 1914.

1599 – GREY IRON
BROADWAY LIMITED BLACK WATER 705 electro-oxidized, twelve wheel style uses eight inboard wheels; 16½" including latch coupler. Variation: (A) white with gold trim; no example seen, but presumably made to go with red combine and blue observation car. Circa 1920.

1600 – GREY-IRON
BROADWAY LIMITED CORINTHIAN 706 electro-oxidized, twelve wheel style uses eight inboard wheels, 15³⁄₈". Variation: (A) painted blue with gold trim. Cataloged 1920.

Most of these coaches were sold with cast iron locomotives and sometimes with pressed steel locomotives.

1601 – HARRIS
Attributed to HARRIS; turquoise blue, 4¹³/₁₆" including coupler tab. Variation: (A) red.

1602 – HARRIS
Blue, outboard wheels, 12 windows, 5⅛". Variation: (A) red.

1603 – WILKINS
Red, black wheels, smooth sides, 4¹³/₁₆". Variation: (A) blue (B) white.

1604 – HARRIS
Attributed to HARRIS; blue with gold trim around windows, inboard wheels, 10 windows, 5¹/₁₆". Variation: (A) red (B) white.

1605 – HARRIS
Attributed to HARRIS (possibly also WILKINS), white, 6⁷/₁₆". Variation: (A) red (B) blue.

1606 – HARRIS
Attributed to HARRIS, red with gold trim, 8⁹/₁₆" (similar, or possibly the same, coaches cataloged by WILKINS in 1905 and 1911).

1607 – BUFFALO
NEW YORK CENTRAL & HUDSON RIVER DEPEW BAGGAGE 1831 rubber stamped in black on red-orange body, brown clerestory roof, black platforms and trucks, heavy gauge steel, steel wheels, 14" including couplers. Circa 1892.

1608 – BUFFALO
NEW YORK CENTRAL & HUDSON RIVER NIAGARA FALLS 819 rubber stamped in black on red-orange body, brown clerestory roof, black platforms and trucks, heavy gauge steel, 14" including couplers, flat steel wheels. Cataloged in 1890 and 1895 lettered only BUFFALO, but no example known. Variation: (A) no lettering, thin gold stripe on roof, wide gold stripe length of sides, iron wheels with four slots. Circa 1892.

1609 – JONES & BIXLER
Attributed to JONES & BIXLER, red with CHICAGO LIMITED rubber stamped in gold, heavy gauge steel, black iron wheels, 13³/₁₆".

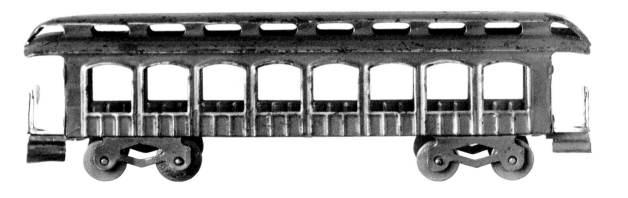

1610 – JONES & BIXLER
Attributed to JONES & BIXLER, red with gold trim, ribbed sides, iron wheels, 13¹/₈". Variation: (A) blue.

Pressed steel cars that were sold in sets with cast iron locomotives and sometimes with steel locos.

1630 – WILKINS
Red with gold trim, black wheels, 5¼" including coupler tabs. Variation: (A) white, (B) blue, (C) red without gold trim. Circa 1905 to 1915.

1631 – WILKINS/KINGSBURY
Red with black wheels, small oval windows by each door, no coupler tabs, 5³/₁₆". Variation: (A) white. Circa 1915 to 1925.

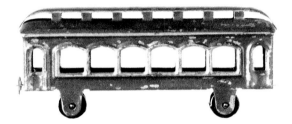

1632 – WILKINS
Red with gold trim, black wheels, 6⅝" including coupler tabs. Circa 1905 to 1911.

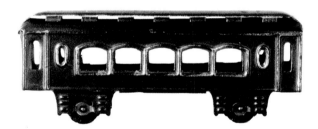

1633 – WILKINS/KINGSBURY
Dark red with gold trim, black wheels, small oval window by each door, no coupler tabs, 7¼". Variation: (A) blue, (B) white. Circa 1916 to 1926.

1634 – WILKINS/KINGSBURY
ERIE RAILROAD rubber stamped in gold, red with black wheels, 10¼". Variation: (A) white, no lettering (B) blue. Circa 1916 to 1926.

1635 – HARRIS
NEW YORK, CHICAGO & BOSTON rubber stamped in black on blue; gold trim around windows. Variation: (A) white (B) red. In 1903 Harris cataloged the same coaches but stamped them NEW YORK CENTRAL & HUDSON RIVER R.R. and listed them in red, white and blue.

1636 – HARRIS
CHICAGO & NORTH WESTERN R.R. 1293 with fancy dingbats, white with black lettering, cast iron wheels. 13¹³/₁₆".

1637 – HARRIS
NEW YORK, CHICAGO & BOSTON LIMITED 1293 with fancy dingbats, rubber stamped in black on red; gold trim around windows, cast iron wheels, 13¹³/₁₆". Variation: (A) blue (also probably made in white). Cataloged in 1903 and 1907 with the number 215.

1638 – HARRIS
LAKE SHORE & MICHIGAN SOUTHERN 1293 rubber stamped in black on blue; gold trim around windows, cast iron wheels, 13¹³/₁₆". Variation: (A) red (B) white.

1639 – UNIDENTIFIED
Red with gold striping, no lettering 13¹⁵/₁₆". Wheels are two-part tin, indicating car was probably pulled by a steel locomotive. The metal stamping is the same as 1636-1638.

1640 WILKINS/KINGSBURY
Red with gold trim, black iron wheels, 13³/₄". Circa 1915-26. The same car was made with one truck that swivels and tin wheels, to be pulled by a pressed steel locomotive.

Pressed steel cars that were sold in sets with cast iron locomotives and sometimes sold with steel locos.

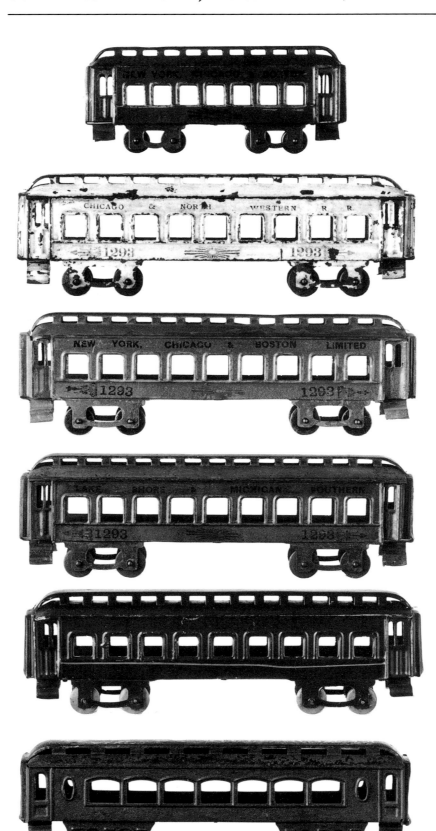

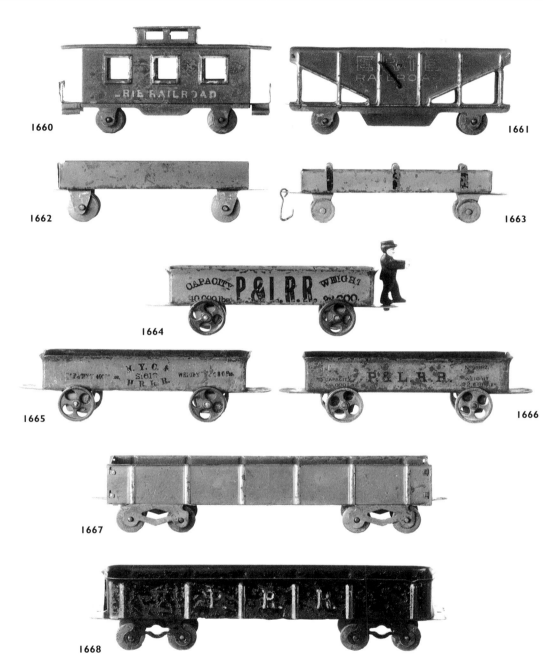

1662 – HUBLEY
All red, iron wheels, 7¹¹/₁₆". Cataloged by HUBLEY in 1921. Variation: (A) all yellow (B) cataloged about 1922, rubber stamped with **U.S. ARTILLERY**, presumably on olive green, with a load of either barrels and boxes or a cannon.

1663 – BUFFALO
Red with black stakes, heavy gauge steel, steel wheels, 7⁵/₈". Variation: (A) yellow, may have been sold under the XL LINE (B) all red without black stakes. Circa 1890 to 1896. An 1892 catalog illustration shows this gondola lettered N.Y.C. & H.R.R.R., no example known.

1664 – BUFFALO
Heavy gauge steel, **P.&L. R.R. CAPACITY** 10,000 lbs. **WEIGHT 22,000** rubber stamped in black on red (the P.&L. no doubt stands for PRATT & LETCHWORTH, the manufacturer of BUFFALO brand toys), iron wheels japanned. The platforms are slotted on both ends to receive separate cast iron brakemen, 8¹¹/₁₆". Variation: (A) yellow body, large N.Y.C.&H.R.R.R. (only), black wheels, may have been sold under the XL brand. Circa 1890 to 1896.

1665 – BUFFALO
Same as 1664 except for lettering N.Y.C.&H.R.R.R. 21619 CAPACITY 40000 lbs. WEIGHT 19580 lbs. Circa 1892.

1666 – BUFFALO
Same as 1664 except for lettering **P.&L.R.R.** CAPACITY 40,000 lbs. NO 1892 WEIGHT 22,600 lbs.

1667 – JONES & BIXLER
Attributed to JONES & BIXLER, red with gold stakes, cast iron wheels, 12³/₁₆".

1668 – HARRIS
P.R.R., black with gold lettering and stakes, cast iron wheels, 12¼". Cataloged in 1903 with a 4-4-0 cast iron locomotive, steel tender and two or three gondolas or two gondolas and a cast iron caboose. Catalog artwork is obviously mixed pieces cut up and repasted together, suggesting that they were not originally intended to be sold with an iron caboose and possibly with another engine and tender.

1660 – WILKINS/KINGSBURY
ERIE RAILROAD rubber stamped in gold on red, gold trim around windows, black iron wheels, 7½" long. Circa 1915 to 1926. The WILKINS 1916 catalog illustration shows this caboose lettered **CGWRR**.

1661 – WILKINS/KINGSBURY
ERIE RAILROAD rubber stamped in gold on red, black iron wheels, side lever operates dumping bay doors, 7¹¹/₁₆". Variation: (A) blue. Circa 1911 to 1926.

4⅝" SERIES

6" FREIGHT SERIES

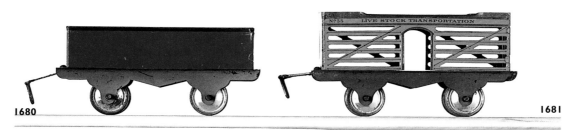

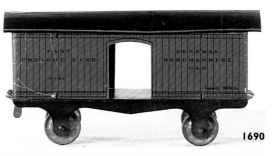

1680 – Gondola, red body, grey chassis, 4⅝". Variation: (A) green body.

1681 – No. 55 LIVE STOCK TRANSPORTATION, green litho on yellow body, grey chassis, (missing grey roof) 4⅝".

1682 – LIMITED VESTIBULE EXPRESS UNITED STATES MAIL BAGGAGE CAR EXPRESS SERVICE NO. 50, red on ivory, grey chassis, grey roof, 4⅝".

1683 – FAST FREIGHT LINE MERCHANDISE CAR NO. 53, green litho on yellow body, grey chassis, green roof, 4⅝".

1684 – LIMITED VESTIBULE EXPRESS BROOKLYN NO. 51, red and black litho on metallic tin body, grey chassis, (green roof repainted), 4⅝". Variation: (A) red and black litho on ivory body, grey chassis, green roof.

1685 – LIMITED VESTIBULE EXPRESS BUFFALO NO. 52, silver litho on deep green background, gold metallic trim around windows, grey chassis, grey roof, 4⅝".

1686 – Caboose (not shown), FAST FREIGHT LINE CABOOSE NO. 156 in black on cream body, black frame.

1687 – IVES Gondola, dark olive chassis, cream body, 6". Variation: (A) medium grey body, light grey chassis.

1688 – NO. 66 TANK LINE, grey chassis, cream body, brown bands, red ends, 6".

1689 – LIVE STOCK TRANSPORTATION, red body with black litho, grey roof and chassis, 6³/₁₆". Variation: (A) black litho on grey body, olive chassis, roof color not known. Circa 1910-12.

1690 – FAST FREIGHT LINE GENERAL MERCHANDISE CAR NO. 64, red body with black litho, dark olive roof and chassis, 6³/₁₆". Variation: (A) black litho on tan body, grey chassis, red roof.

1691 – FAST FREIGHT CABOOSE NO. 126, red-orange body with black litho, apple green roof, dark green chassis, dark olive cupola, red-orange roof on cupola, 6¹/₁₆". Variation: (A) brown litho on cream body, chassis grey, and roof of cupola green (B) brown litho on cream body, chassis olive, roof and cupola dark green, red roof on cupola.

1710 – UNITED STATES MAIL BAGGAGE CAR NUMBER 60, ivory body with burnt red litho, grey chassis, grey roof, 6¹/₁₆". Variation: (A) green roof (B) olive green chassis, dark green roof.

1712 – LIMITED VESTIBULE EXPRESS PRINCESS gold litho on navy blue body, grey chassis and roof, 6¹/₁₆". Variation: (A) brown litho on ivory body, olive chassis, dark green roof.

1713 – LIMITED VESTIBULE EXPRESS EMPRESS litho on metallic tin, grey chassis, tan-grey roof, 6¹/₁₆". Variation: (A) black litho on red body, olive chassis, dark green roof (B) yellow lettering, anodized blue around windows, bronze body, grey chassis and roof.

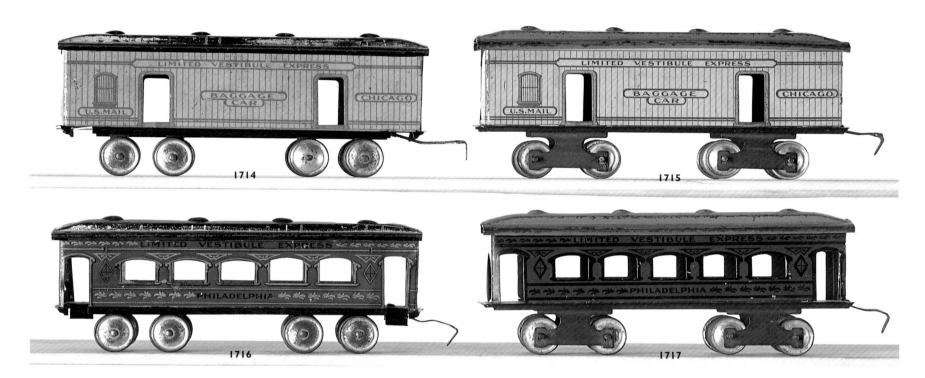

1714 – LIMITED VESTIBULE EXPRESS
U.S. MAIL BAGGAGE CAR CHICAGO in
brown litho on ivory background; black
frame, black roof with silver trim, outboard wheels, 8$\frac{1}{8}$". Circa pre-1910.
From a private collection

1716 – LIMITED VESTIBULE EXPRESS
PHILADELPHIA in black and gold litho on
green: black frame, black roof with
silver trim, outboard wheels; 8$\frac{1}{8}$".
Circa pre-1910.
From a private collection

1715 – LIMITED VESTIBULE EXPRESS
U.S. MAIL BAGGAGE CAR CHICAGO in
brown litho on ivory background; olive
frame, grey roof, inboard wheels,
8$\frac{5}{16}$". Cataloged 1910-12.
From a private collection

1717 – LIMITED VESTIBULE EXPRESS
PHILADELPHIA in black on green body;
olive frame, grey roof, inboard trucks,
8$\frac{5}{16}$". Cataloged 1910-12.
From a private collection

1730 – Baggage and express **No. 70**, red litho, yellow background, grey chassis, grey roof, black trucks, inboard wheels, 11". Circa 1910-12.

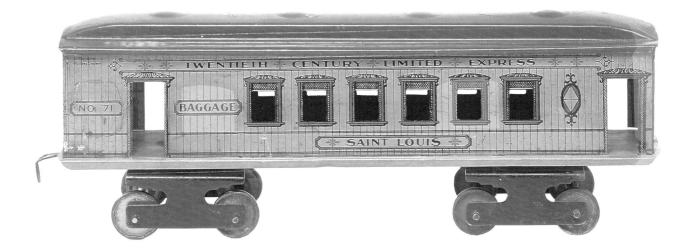

1731 – No. 71 combination car, red litho on yellow background, grey chassis, green roof, black trucks, inboard wheels, 11". Circa 1910-12.

1732 – No. 72 drawing room car, red litho on yellow background, grey chassis, green roof, black trucks, inboard wheels, 11". Circa 1910-12.
All cars from a private collection
DICK KAPLAN PHOTO

1760 – KILGORE
Blue, nickelplated, inboard wheels. Part of the BILLY BOY RAILROAD TOY SET, 4³/₈". Variation (A) red. Circa 1930.

1761 – UNIDENTIFIED
A highly unusual and unidentified box car with a complicated assembly of 7 separate castings: the two sides, two doors and interior track for the doors at both top and bottom and the assembly for the one truck that pivots. The flat wheels are of steel. The coupler tang from the pivoting truck is broken off. Paint is a faded red, 5¹⁵/₁₆".

1762

1763

1764

1766

1762 – IDEAL
WABASH R.R. CAPACITY **40,000 lbs.**, nickelplated, solid floor, 11¾".. Variation: (A) four ½" and two ¼" holes in the floor (B) one side with solid floor, the other with floor holes. Circa 1899.

1763 – IDEAL
MERCHANTS' DESPATCH CAPACITY **40,000 lbs.**, nickelplated, solid wheels, 11¾". Variation: (A) electro-oxidized (B) red (C) tuscan. Circa 1903.

1764 – ARCADE
MERCHANTS' DESPATCH CAPACITY **40,000 lbs.**, red with gold lettering; identical to 1763 by IDEAL except for being ¼" shorter and using the five-hole wheels, 11⁷⁄₁₆". Variation: (A) nickelplated. Cataloged as nickelplated. Cataloged 1902-17.

1765 – WILKINS
MERCHANTS DESPATCH FAST FREIGHT **4** rubber stamped in gold on red; gold highlights on trucks, articulated trucks. Lettering was sometimes varnished over, leaving a darker color background while the rest of the paint job shows normal fading, 13⅛". Variation: (A) red-orange, gold highlights on trucks, two small holes in one end of roof for a standing brakeman (B) red-orange, number **4**, no highlights on trucks, two holes for brakeman (C) tuscan, hand lettered CHESHIRE R.R. in gold, no holes in roof (D) tuscan, hand lettered MERCHANT (singular) DESPATCH FAST FREIGHT in white, no roof holes (E) tuscan, rubber stamped MERCHANTS DESPATCH FAST FREIGHT in gold (generally well faded), no roof holes (F) tuscan, hand lettered MERCHANTS DESPATCH (in one line) (FAST FREIGHT) in gold, no roof holes (G) tuscan, hand lettered BOSTON & MAINE, no roof holes.

1766 – IVES
UNION LINE CAPACITY **50,000 lbs.**, dark brown with gold lettering, red wheels, 13⅝". Variation: (A) mustard brown (B) red-orange, yellow wheels. Cataloged by IVES in 1893 at $13.50 a dozen.

1780 – KILGORE
Red, nickelplated inboard wheels, **KILGORE** embossed inside one side, 4¹/₁₆".

1781 – HUBLEY
Deep red, no moving parts, **72** embossed on bottom, 3¹¹/₁₆" (may also been sold by JONES & BIXLER).

1782 – IVES
Red with japanned wheels, one-piece casting, 4". Variation: (A) black with yellow wheels (B) black with japanned wheels. Circa 1893-1904.

1783 – HUBLEY
Red, one-piece casting, **205** stamped inside bottom, axles crimped on both ends, 4⁵/₁₆". Circa 1910.

1784 – WILKINS
Red. This example has one pair of red wheels and one pair of black wheels (appears original), single center rivet, 3⁷/₈". Circa 1891.

1785 – IDEAL
Attributed to IDEAL, Tuscan with gold stakes, one-piece casting, appears identical to 1782 but ¹/₈" smaller at 3⁷/₈". Variation: (A) nickelplated. Cataloged with a 150 locomotive. Circa 1902 (may have also been sold by ARCADE).

1786 – JONES & BIXLER
Attributed to JONES & BIXLER, yellow, one-piece casting, **76** embossed on bottom, wheels on this example may not be original, 5⁵/₁₆". Cataloged by JONES & BIXLER in 1912.

1787 – DENT
Red, stakes painted gold, single center rivet, 4³/₈". Variation: (A) blue with gold stakes.

1788 – ATTRIBUTED TO HARRIS
White, one-piece casting, 5½". Variation: (A) red (B) blue.

1789 – KENTON
Nickelplated, single center rivet, 5¼". Cataloged by KENTON in 1914 and 1923.

1780   1781   1782

1783   1784   1785

1786   1787

1788   1789

1790   1791

1792   1793

1790 – IDEAL
Attributed to IDEAL (possibly also sold by ARCADE); originally nickelplated, one-piece casting, 5½". Variation: (A) trucks flat with sides, red, gold stakes, black wheels, 5⁹/₁₆", manufacturer unidentified. Circa 1899 to 1923.

1791 – KENTON
Attributed to KENTON, original finish undetermined, single center rivet, inboard wheels, 5³/₁₆".

1792 – DENT
Blue, single center rivet, inboard wheels, 5½". Circa 1930.

1793 – GREY IRON
40, nickelplated, single center rivet, 5¹/₁₆".

1794

1795

1796

1797

1798

1799

1800

1801

1794 – CLIMAX
UPRR, yellow with red wheels, end rivets, 5¹³/₁₆". Variation: (A) blue with red wheels. Circa 1897.

1795 – IDEAL
M.C.R.R., nickelplated, end rivets, 6¹/₁₆". Variation: (A) 5¹³/₁₆", red, attributed to CLIMAX. Circa 1895 to 1902.

1796 – ARCADE
(possibly also sold by IDEAL)
M.C.R.R., nickelplated, single center rivet, 5¹¹/₁₆". Variation: (A) red.

1797 – CLIMAX
M.C.R.R., nickelplated, single center rivet, 5⁹/₁₆". Note wheel ridges are a bit flatter than the comparable model by ARCADE (1796).

1798 – HARRIS
M.C.R.R., blue with gold trim, black wheels, end rivets, 6¹/₄".

1799 – DENT
M.C.R.R., blue with gold trim, single center rivet, 5³/₄". Variation: (A) white, (B) red.

1800 – A. C. WILLIAMS
USA, all black, 4³/₈" including latch coupler.

1801 – A. C. WILLIAMS
USA, black with red wheels, 5¹/₈" including latch coupler.

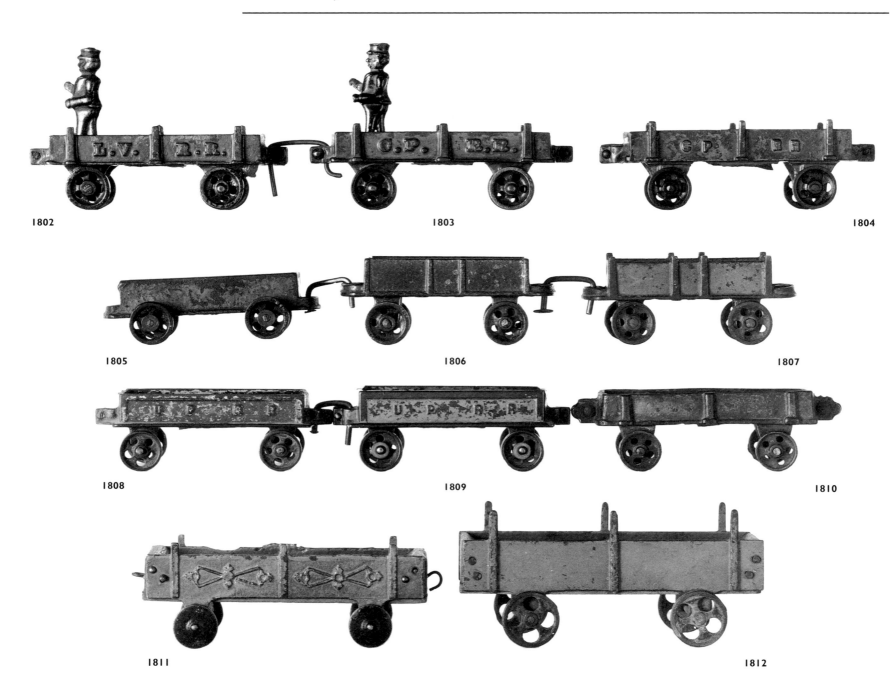

1802

1803

1804

1805

1806

1807

1808

1809

1810

1811

1812

1802 – IVES
L.V.R.R., red with japanned wheels, floor slotted at one end for separate cast iron figure. 5¹³/₁₆".

1803 – IVES
C.P.R.R., red with japanned wheels, separate cast iron figure, 6". Cataloged by IVES in 1893 and 1904.

1804 – ATTRIBUTED TO IVES
CPRR, red, wheels usually black, may be japanned, has a shelf with a slot inside one end to receive a separate standing figure. This shelf is similar to that on the STEVENS 1808, 6³/₁₆". Variation: (A) no shelf inside, uses coupler pin similar to CARPENTER's (1806).

1805 – CARPENTER
PATENTED MAY.25.1880. REISSUED MARCH 14.1882 embossed in straight lines across the bottom, red with black wheels, 4¹⁵/₁₆". Variation: (A) PATENTED MAY.25.1880 embossed inside the floor in one line. Circa 1880 to 1885.

1806 – CARPENTER
PAT. MAY 25.1880 (reissued) REISS'D MAR.14.82 embossed on the bottom with the first line in an arch. Note narrow stakes do not protrude above edge of sides, red with black wheels, notched at one end for a separate iron brakeman, 4¹⁵/₁₆". Variation: (A) stakes protrude above edges, nipple on floor by notch for figure. Circa 1880 to 1890.

1807 – CARPENTER
PAT. MAY 25.1880 (reissued) REISS'D MAR.14.82 embossed on the bottom, first line is arched. Note wider stakes protruding above top edge of siding, red with black wheels, notched at one end for a separate iron brakeman, 4⅞".

1808 – STEVENS
UPRR, red sides, light green inside, has a narrow slotted shelf inside one end probably to hold a standing figure, 5⅜".

1809 – STEVENS
UPRR, red sides, light green inside, no slot or shelf inside; sides are ⅞" tall, ⅛" taller than 1808, length is the same at 5⅜".

1810 – HARRIS
Attributed to HARRIS, red, 6⅛".

1811 – WELKER & CROSBY
Red with black wheels, sides and wheels are cast iron, floor and ends are wood, 6⁵⁄₁₆" not counting wire couplers. Variation: (A) tuscan.

1812 – WELKER & CROSBY
Red with black wheels, sides and wheels are cast iron, floor and ends are wood, 6¹³⁄₁₆".

1813

1814

1815

1816

1817

1813 – KENTON
Red, single center rivet. 7¹⁄₁₆"

1814 – JONES & BIXLER
LVRR, red, single center rivet, inboard wheels (the correct wheels would be larger in diameter than the replacements shown); **77** embossed inside each side, 6⅝". Variation: (A) dark green, gold letters.

1815 – CARPENTER
Attributed to CARPENTER; red with black wheels, wood floor, end rivets, 8⅛".

1816 – JONES & BIXLER
Red, single center rivet, **78** embossed inside each side, 8⅛". Variation: (A) 7¹³⁄₁₆", no number inside. Circa 1912.

1817 – DENT
Red with gold stakes, end rivets, 7⁷⁄₁₆". Variation: (A) white (B) blue with gold stakes. Circa 1907.

1830

1834

1831

1835

1832

1836

1833

1837

1830 – BUFFALO
Red with steel wheels, single center rivet. 5$^{15}/_{16}$".

1831 – WILKINS
Red with black wheels, single center rivet, two holes in floor to receive a separate cast iron figure, 6". Cataloged by WILKINS in 1895.

1832 – WILKINS
Body is cast in one solid piece, no rivets. C embossed on bottom; two holes in floor to receive separate cast iron figure, 6$^1/_8$". Variation: (A) no holes in floor. Circa 1892-95.

1833 – KENTON
Red with gold stakes, black wheels; wheels towards the end move, wheels towards the center are fixed, 6$^1/_2$". Variation: (A) all red. Cataloged by KENTON in 1914 and 1923.

1834 – IDEAL
C.R.I.&P.R.R., nickelplated, single center rivet. 6".

1835 – ATTRIBUTED TO IDEAL
M.C.R.R., red, wheels and lettering on this example are overpainted blue which is presumed to be original, single center rivet, 6$^3/_{16}$".

1836 – IDEAL
M.C.R.R., nickelplated, end rivets, wide shoulder on coupler, 6$^5/_8$". Variation: (A) painted red-orange with yellow wheels.

1837 – IDEAL
M.C.R.R., nickelplated, end rivets, straight shoulders on couplers, 6$^5/_8$". Variation: (A) painted red-orange with yellow wheels. Circa 1895-99.

1838 – KENTON

Tan with gold stakes, floor notched at each end to receive a standing figure, trucks are flat and smooth, 8⁷/₈". Variation: (A) all red.

1839 – KENTON

Red with gold stakes, gold trim on trucks, black wheels, horizontal ridges on trucks, floor slotted at each end for a standing figure, 8⁷/₈". Variation: (A) no gold trim. Cataloged by KENTON in 1914 and 1923.

1840 – IVES

Red with bare metal wheels, T trucks, floor slotted at one end for a standing figure, 8⁷/₈". Cataloged by IVES in 1893 and 1904.

1841 – IVES

Red, small wheels on vertical truck mounts, floor not slotted for a figure, 8⁷/₈".

1842 – WILKINS

CAPACITY 50,000 LBS. NO. 1888 WT. 48,100, painted black overall with the sides and wheels overpainted red, couplers have a lower profile but a wider shoulder than 1843, 8¹¹/₁₆". Cataloged by WILKINS in 1895.

1843 – WILKINS

CAPACITY 50,000 LBS NO. 1888 WT. 48,100, red with black wheels, coupler has a taller profile than 1842, but lacks the wider shoulder, 8³/₄". Variation: (A) green.

1844

1845   1846

1847   1848

1849   1850

1851   1852

1844 – IDEAL
Attributed to IDEAL, M.C.R.R., all red with gold letters, end rivets, axle rivets peened on both ends, 8¹³/₁₆". Variation: (A) red with black wheels (B) nickelplated.

1845 – JONES & BIXLER
UPRR blue with gold wheels, single center rivet, 8⁹/₁₆". Variation: (A) red with gold wheels. (Casting is the same as 1846 by CLIMAX only the wheels are different.)

1846 – CLIMAX
UPRR, nickelplated, single center rivet. Circa 1897, 8⁹/₁₆".

1847 – HARRIS
MCRR, yellow with black wheels, gold letters, end rivets, 9¹/₁₆". Variation: (A) painted red (B) nickelplated. Circa 1903.

1848 – JONES & BIXLER
MCRR, red with gold wheels, end rivets, 8⁷/₈". Variation: (A) green with gold lettering and stakes. Cataloged by JONES & BIXLER in 1912.

1849 – IDEAL
M.C.R.R., nickelplated, single center rivet, 8³/₄". Variation: (A) painted red (B) electro-oxidized (C) 8½", red, black wheels, gold on letters, unidentified. Same size as ARCADE and JONES & BIXLER.

1850 – IDEAL
M.C.R.R., nickelplated, end rivets. Circa 1895-1907, 9¹/₈".

1851 – DENT
M.C.R.R., red-orange, 8¹³/₁₆". Variation: (A) 8¹¹/₁₆", red, casting ridges on bottom are ground off smooth, (B) blue, (C) white. Circa 1907.

1852 – ARCADE
C.R.I.&P.R.R., nickelplated, single center rivet, 8½".

Most of these gondolas (1853-1856) have a small rectangular slot in the floor towards each end; some have one slot, a few none. The slot is presumably for a standing figure. The only figure I've seen fit in the slot is a BUFFALO brakeman.

1853 – HARRIS
H.T.R.R., red with gold stakes, black wheels, 9⅛".

1854 – HARRIS
H.T.R.R. CAPACITY 40000 LBS. WEIGHT 23500 LBS., red with gold stakes, black wheels, 9⁷/₁₆".

1855 – HARRIS
C.B.&Q.R.R. CAPACITY 40000 LBS. WEIGHT 23500 LBS., red with gold stakes, black wheels, 9⁷/₁₆".

1856 – ATTRIBUTED TO HARRIS
L.V.R.R., no paint on this example but presumed to have been red with black wheels, 9³/₁₆". Casting is thick and heavy; wheels are unusually thick and crude—possibly not original to this piece, but aged with it.

1857 – WILKINS
Red-orange, usually with two holes drilled on the outside lip of one end where a brakeman could stand, 14⅛". Variation: (A) tuscan. Circa 1892-95.

1870   1871

1872   1873

1874   1875

1870 – KENTON
DL&W, red with gold trim, pin couplers, only the wheels towards the ends move, 6⁹/₁₆". The KENTON 1914 to 1923 catalogs show this car, but illustrated as a larger hopper.

1871 – HUBLEY
PENN R.R. P.R.R. 1100, olive green with gold lettering, dump doors and wheel nickelplated. About 7" long not including latch coupler. The olive color was listed in 1930 with only one car per set. Variation: (A) black, cataloged

from 1917 to 1929 with two or three cars in a set. In 1917 it was illustrated with pin couplers. Circa 1917 to 1932.

1872 – HUBLEY
PENNSYLVANIA PRR 3000 black with gold lettering, pin couplers, only wheels towards each end move, 9⁵/₈". Circa 1917 to 1919.

1873 – HUBLEY
PENNSYLVANIA PRR 3000, black with gold trim, 9⁵/₈" not including latch coupler. Circa 1920.

1874 – JONES & BIXLER (KENTON)
CRR, black with gold trim, white circle around a red dot on right end, only wheels towards each end move, pin couplers, 8⁹/₁₆". Cataloged by JONES & BIXLER in 1912. Also cataloged by KENTON in 1914, presumably selling excess J&B inventory.

1875 – DENT
M.C.R.R., red with gold trim, pin couplers, all wheels move, 8¹⁵/₁₆". Variation: (A) black (B) blue (C) white.

1962 – IDEAL
Turquoise blue, 7³/₈".

1963 – WILKINS
CABOOSE rubber stamped in gold on
red-orange; roof has two holes
near the cupola, presumably where a
cast iron brakeman figure would stand,
7¹/₄". It's interesting to note that this is
the only caboose with wheel bearings
based on real 4-wheel equipment.
Cataloged by WILKINS in 1895.

1964 – IDEAL
Tuscan with yellow wheels, 9¹/₄".
Variation: (A) large diameter six-hole
wheels.

GLOSSARY

ATTRIBUTED TO Not a positive identification as to manufacturer, but believed to have been made by or attributed to the manufacturer listed

CIRCA Approximate date

CONNECTING RODS Side rods on a locomotive that deliver the driving power from the steam chest to the drive wheels

COUPLER On most cast iron toy trains, the rectangular form on the end of each car representing the mechanism which on a real train, coupled one car to another. Toy couplers actually hook up with a wire or pin. Some use a latching device called an automatic coupler.

COUPLING PIN A heavy wire mounted in the coupler of one toy to hook to the coupler of another

COUPLING RODS Side rods on a locomotive connecting one drive wheel to the next

DIAPHRAM Accordion-like attachment on the end of passenger coaches which weatherproofs the walkway between cars; called concertina gangways in Europe

DRIVERS OR DRIVING WHEELS The large wheels on a locomotive to which the power is applied

EMBOSSED Numbers or letters raised on the casting

JAPANNED Brown translucent finish of shellack, popular circa 1890 to 1910

PEEN The end of a rivet or axle flattened by a hammer or tool

TUSCAN Reddish-brown brick color

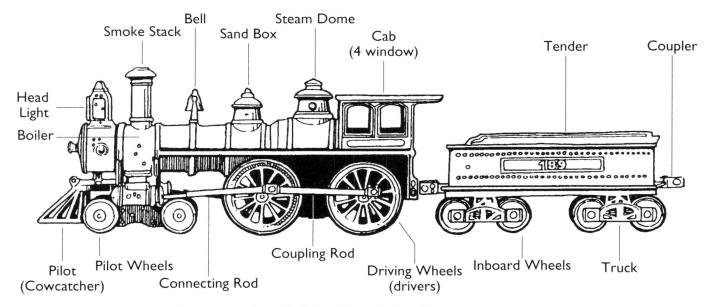

Head Light
Boiler
Smoke Stack
Bell
Sand Box
Steam Dome
Cab (4 window)
Tender
Coupler
Pilot (Cowcatcher)
Pilot Wheels
Connecting Rod
Coupling Rod
Driving Wheels (drivers)
Inboard Wheels
Truck

Locomotive 2-4-0 Wheel Configuration

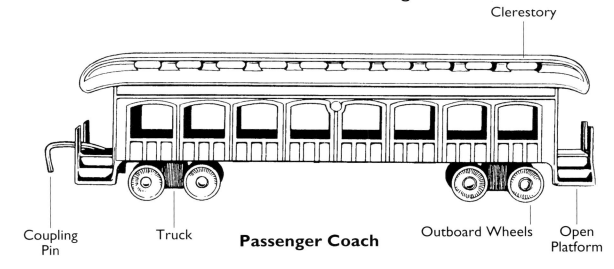

Clerestory
Coupling Pin
Truck
Outboard Wheels
Open Platform

Passenger Coach

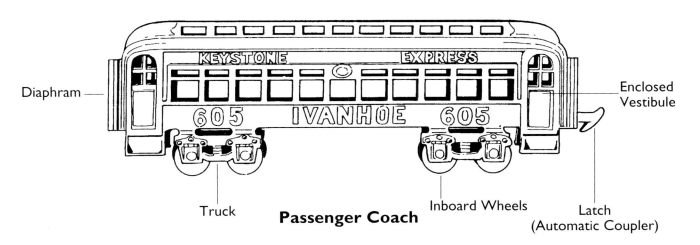

Diaphram
KEYSTONE EXPRESS
605 IVANHOE 605
Enclosed Vestibule
Truck
Inboard Wheels
Latch (Automatic Coupler)

Passenger Coach

FINDING CAST IRON TRAINS

One-stop shopping is out of the question, of course. But the challenge and excitement of the hunt accounts for much of the fun of collecting. Floor trains sometimes show up at estate auctions and are also included from time to time at toy auctions held frequently around the country. Auction houses that often feature toys, and which accept absentee bids and provide illustrated catalogs, include:

Noel Barrett Antiques & Auctions Ltd.
P.O. Box 1001
Carversville, PA 18912
(215) 297-5109
FAX (215) 297-0457

Christie's East
219 E. 67th St.
New York, NY 10021
(212) 606-0400
FAX (212) 737-6076

James D. Julia, Inc.
Box 830
Rt 201, Skowhegan Rd.
Fairfield, ME 04937
(207) 453-7125
FAX (207) 453-2502

Richard Opfer Auctioneering
1919 Greenspring Dr.
Timonium, MD 21093
(410) 252-5035
FAX (410) 252-5863

Lloyd Ralston Toys
173 Post Rd.
Fairfield, CT 06430
(203) 255-1233
FAX (203) 256-9094

Sotheby's
1334 York Ave.
New York, NY 10021
(212) 606-7424
FAX (212) 606-7249

Check also the monthly magazine *Antique Toy World*, which advertises toys sales and auctions and lists most of the toy swap meets.

Antique Toy World
4419 W. Irving Park Rd.
Chicago, IL 60641
(312) 725-0633
FAX (312)725-3449

RARITY & PRICE GUIDE
TO CAST IRON FLOOR TRAINS

ales of cast iron floor trains are so infrequent and prices vary so greatly that a listing of values will inherently be grossly inaccurate. So with the thought that a price guide of estimates from a collector with 10 years experience of buying cast iron floor trains at toy and train meets, auctions, and from private parties is better than no price guide at all, I make the following attempt.

Values are greatly affected by condition. A rusted or broken toy may be worth only a fraction of one in very good original condition. A toy in excellent condition is the exception and may command a considerably higher price. The ultimate selling price is determined by a willing seller and a willing buyer.

Sets: the value of a train set is approximately the sum total of its individual components.

Original boxes: either wood or cardboard are rare and add substantially to the value of a train, perhaps 50%.

Values listed are for VERY GOOD original condition with 80% or more original paint, or plating, no cracks, no breaks, no repairs, no repaint, no parts missing, and no heavy rust. Locomotives include tenders and street cars include horses, unless specified otherwise.

CODE	RARITY
NCS	No Confirmed Sighting
XR	Extremely Rare
R	Rare
S	Scarce
L	Limited
C	Common
MC	Most Common

The cars in sets 520, 521 and 522 are referred to by their set number as they are not pictured separately. All other cars, locomotives, etc., are photographed individually and given a separate number.

No.		Rarity	Price $
520	Gondola, orange	S	200
520	Gondola, copper	R	250
520	Gondola, gold, disk wheels	R	250
520	Coach, copper	XR	400
520	Coach, orange	R	350
521	Merchandise car, orange	XR	300
521	Merchandise car, copper	XR	300
522	Gondola	R	300
522	Merchandise car	XR	400
620		L	40
621		XR	75
622		XR	75
622A		R	50
623		R	50
623A		XR	75
623B		XR	75
623C		XR	75
624		R	50
625		R	50
626		L	60
626A		XR	75
627		R	60
628		XR	75
629		XR	75
629A		R	65
630	With steel coach	XR	100
631		R	75
631A		R	75
632		XR	100
633		R	150
634		XR	150
635		S	100
635A		R	125
636		R	125
636A		R	125

CODE	RARITY
NCS	No Confirmed Sighting
XR	Extremely Rare
R	Rare
S	Scarce
L	Limited
C	Common
MC	Most Common

No.		Rarity	Price $
637		XR	175
637A		XR	175
638		XR	150
638A		XR	150
638B		XR	150
639		XR	175
640		XR	175
640A		XR	150
641		XR	250
642		XR	250
643		R	250
644		XR	250
645		XR	150
646		S	100
646A		R	125
647		C	75
648		XR	300
649		XR	200
650		R	175
650A		XR	200
651		S	250
652		XR	250
653		R	150
654		R	150
655		S	150
656		R	150
656A		XR	175
657		R	150
657A		XR	150
658		XR	175
658A		R	150
658B		S	125
659		XR	300
660		XR	175
661		L	150
661A		XR	225
662		XR	225
663		L	150
663A		XR	175
664		S	50
665		S	50
665A		R	60
666		L	40
667		XR	125
667A		C	40
667B		S	45
668		XR	150
669		XR	150

No.		Rarity	Price $
669A		L	75
670		L	75
670A		R	90
671		XR	15
672		XR	150
673		S	100
674		S	100
675		XR	150
675A		XR	150
676		S	100
677		L	150
677A		S	150
677B		XR	175
678		R	175
679		S	100
680		L	75
680A		XR	150
681		XR	150
681A		L	100
681B		R	125
682		R	125
682A		R	125
683		XR	150
684		XR	125
684A		XR	125
684B		XR	125
685		XR	75
686		R	125
686A		XR	150
687		XR	150
687A		XR	150
687B		XR	150
688		XR	150
688A		XR	150
689		R	125
689A		XR	150
690		XR	150
691		XR	150
710		S	75
710A		R	90
711		S	75
711A		S	75
711B		XR	100
712		C	50
713		L	65
740		S	400
741		XR	500
742	No tender	L	75

No.		Rarity	Price $
743		C	150
744	No tender	R	150
744A	No tender	XR	200
745		XR	300
746		S	75
747		S	150
747A		R	175
748		L	300
749		R	750
750		L	350
751		XR	700
752		XR	450
753	Not a confirmed set		
754		XR	500
754A		XR	500
755		S	350
755A		XR	400
756		R	400
756A	Not a confirmed set		
757		C	500
758		R	650
759		S	550
760		XR	1,500
761		L	400
762		XR	500
763		R	500
764		R	600
765	No tender	XR	700
765	With tender	XR	1,200
765A	No tender	XR	700
765A	With tender	XR	1,200
766		C	500
766A		R	600
767		XR	1,000
768		L	500
769		L	500
769A		XR	600
770		XR	900
771		XR	1,000
800		S	600
801		S	700
802		XR	400
802A		XR	450
803		C	275
804		XR	2,000
820		S	150
821		XR	250
821A		XR	250